10374

Editor: Andreas Bayias
Translation: H.L. Turner, Klio Panourgias
Plans: Dimos Svolopoulos
Cover Design: R.V. Graphics
Photography: Ilias Iliadis, P. Mylonas, Annivas Stamatopoulos
DTP: Spyridoula Vonitsi
Colour separation-films: EUROGRAPH MICHAÏLIDIS BROS Ltd.

Printed and bound in Greece

ISBN 978-960-89451-2-8

The map on page 5, the photographs and drawings on pages 16, 18b, 20, 21a, 22, 29, 31, 35a, b, 36, 37a-c, 38a, 46, 50b, 57a, 69b, 117a, 118a-b, as well as the reconstructions on the fold-out at the end of the book come from the archive of the French Archaeological School in Athens.

Dr. FOTINI ZAPHIROPOULOU
HON. CURATOR OF ANTIQUITIES

DELOS
MONUMENTS AND MUSEUM

KRENE EDITIONS

ATHENS 2013

MYTH – HISTORY

Delos is a thin strip of land protruding from the sea with rock formations of slate, gneiss, and granite, characteristic of the Cycladic region. The gneiss, in particular, reflects the light despite its earthly colour. The length of Delos from north to south does not exceed 5 kms while its width is 1.3 kms. During the rainy season, numerous small rivulets trickle down its low hills, separated by narrow valleys, to the sea. A single torrent, the Inopos, has a relatively steady flow from south to north. It springs from south of Mt. Cynthus and flows along the island's western side to a valley near the harbour. Its waters were collected in a ravine quite high up in the foothills of Cynthus (see p. 64). Delos does not have a shortage of drinking water; a layer of limestone, which in some places covers the granite surface, retains sufficient quantities of rainwater. Thus the island's wells supplied its inhabitants with adequate reserves.

The only significant elevation on this otherwise flat area of land is Mt. Cynthus, a peak of pure granite located roughly at the island's centre. This is the sacred Delian mountain that dominates its surroundings, not because of its height (112 m), but because it contrasts sharply with its low-lying and flat surroundings. The island's shores, buffeted by strong winds and waves, border the mountain's base. Rugged rocks, particularly to the north, but also the lunar-like southern tip, Cherronissos, open out in serpentine formations to create small bays: Gourna to the northeast, the port nearest to Mykonos, Scardanas to the northwest, and Fournoi to the south-southwest of the island. Finally, half way down the west coast is the ancient sacred harbour, which offers safe mooring for boats thanks to the two rocks, called Mikros and Megalos Rematiaris, in the channel between Delos and Rheneia. Here, close to the harbour, is the island's principal valley, which passes through hills and extends to the northeast, almost to the bay of Gourna. Its northernmost part once flooded and formed the Sacred Lake.

Greater Delos, i.e. ancient Rheneia, is formed by the continuation to the west of Lesser Delos, as its inhabitants refer presently to the two islands. Flatter and wider, double in length and width, with larger and safer bays and more cultivable land, Rheneia has the most inhabitants of the two today.

Delos' geographical location is key; it is located roughly at the centre of the Cyclades and halfway along the maritime route from mainland Greece to Ionia, the eastern islands of Chios, Samos, Rhodes and Crete. It was only natural that Delos quickly became a commercial harbour, which later developed into one of the most important ports in the eastern Mediterranean.

A major factor in Delos' great success was that it was considered sacred ground - the birthplace of Apollo, a major Greek deity. The myth connected to his birth is well known.

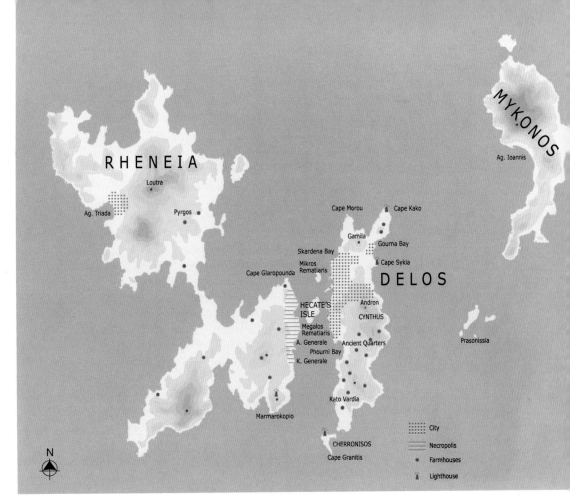

Map of Delos and Rheneia.

When Zeus' affair with the Titan Leto left her pregnant, Hera's jealousy turned into a merciless pursuit of her rival. Leto could not find a safe place to give birth to her child until she managed to find a piece of floating rock jutting from the sea. There she decided to stop despite the fear in her heart. She remained there after promising that the island would cease its wanderings and stay in one place, and that the child born there would never abandon it and would bring it great glory and wealth. This is what happened. Leto's painful labour lasted for nine days because Hera prevented Eileithyia, goddess of childbirth, from coming to her aid. Finally, other goddesses who supported Leto sent Iris, the messenger of the gods, to fetch Eileithyia after secretly promising her the gift a necklace. After this, Leto, "looking towards Cynthus, the mountain of Zeus" and near the "wheel-shaped" lake, gave birth to the most beautiful of the immortals. The land, bathed in radiant light and carpeted with flowers, rejoiced as the newborn Phoebus with his long hair threw off his swaddling clothes and began wandering with his favourite lyre and bow. Henceforth, the island Asteria, known up until then as A-delos, the 'invisible' because of its perpetual wandering, became known as Delos, meaning 'clearly seen'. Legend has it that it was held fast by adamantine chains.

Most importantly, however, Delos became one of the most important and venerated sacred places of ancient Greece.

Apollo, the young and most distinctive of the Olympian gods introduced by the new populations who inhabited the Greek world, had two personalities: in remote and mountainous Delphi he was the vengeful god who decided the fate of mortals on a private but also public level through his all-powerful oracle, in Delos he was the god of light and music, of the joy of life in general; here he hated anything that might pollute the cleanliness and purity of his island, including the birth and death of those who lived there, who had to be born and to die elsewhere. Apollo remained absolutely dominant on sacred Delos and was worshipped until later years as part of the Apollonian Trinity - with his sister Artemis and his mother Leto - as shown by numerous surviving votive inscriptions.

The oldest traces of habitation on Delos come from the middle of the 3rd millennium BC. These first settlers must have belonged to one of the prehistoric peoples of the Aegean, which Thucydides calls Carians. Remains of their circular dwellings/huts were found high on Mt. Cynthus, the safest place on the island. During the following millennium however, as on other Cycladic islands, there is no trace of human presence.

The sacred island of Apollo first flourished during the Mycenaean period (1580-1200 BC), after the middle of the 2nd millennium. The town spread down into the fertile valley while a settlement with important buildings developed around the central harbour.

Around 1100 BC, the Mycenaean world gave way to the Ionians who flooded out of mainland Greece to settle on the islands and the eastern shores of the Mediterranean. The *Odyssey* and the Homeric *Hymn to Apollo*, written around 700 BC (according to some scholars, the *Hymn to Apollo* was written during the 2nd half of the 7th century BC), mention Delos as a renowned Ionian holy centre. Naturally, boats full of pilgrims also brought merchandise and Delos flourished as a commercial port since then. It is important to note that the "great synod" of the Ionians was a particular declaration of worship in a common sacred centre where they came together driven by common interests and aims.

When a place acquires a reputation as an important religious centre, many other cities wishing to claim spiritual dominance tend to appear. A place of religious radiance can also have significant political influence. The Naxians were among the first Ionians who tried to impose their control, at least on a cultural level, over the holy island and, through it, over the rest of the Cyclades. After the middle of the 7th century BC, for about a century, they presented numerous votive offerings and adorned the sanctuary of Apollo with important buildings. During the 6th century BC, Paros also attempted to gain influence with many votive offerings. At the same time the tyrant of Samos, Polycrates, achieved naval control in the central eastern Aegean and over several islands including Rheneia, which Thucydides mentions he offered to the Delian Apollo by joining it to Delos with a chain. This event was only the beginning of Rheneia's permanent subordination to the Apollonian shrine, which throughout its long history kept a large area of the island under its control, its cultivable areas being Delos's main source of nourishment. It was the Athenians, however, who, from early on, wanted to assert control over Delos, Ionia and the islands of the Aegean. Athenian influence on Delos was first attested during the reign of the tyrant Peisistratos who erected an archaic temple to Apollo and ordered the first purification of Delos during his third tyranny, 540-528 BC. This purification called for all graves from that part of the island visible from the temple of Apollo to be removed. After the fall of Peisistratos and the start of the Persian wars (490 BC), during which the Asian invaders respected the island's sanctity, Athenian influence ceased. At the same time, however, the great Theorias (religious festivals) lost their splendour because the Ionians of Asian Minor and its neighboring islands came under Persian rule and the Ionian amphictiony on Delos was dissolved. After the victory of the Greeks over the Persians, which was largely thanks to the Athenians, Athens took over the leadership of the Greek city-states once again and in 478 BC established the first Athenian League with the participation of almost all of the Aegean Greek city-states. The Athenian League's seat was in Delos, where they placed the Treasury containing the common levies. Once again, Delos became the centre of the Ionian amphictiony, but was under the direct influence of Athens since the Athenian amphictions assumed responsibility for the sanctuary, despite Delos having local rulers, called the 'neochors'. Gradually, the league became an Athenian hegemony and in 456 BC the Treasury was moved to the Athenian Acropolis for greater safety. The Athenians decided to conduct a second purification of Delos in the winter of 426/5 BC after the plague caused by the Peloponnesian War and on the advice of an oracle. Delians were forbidden not only to die, but also to be born on the sacred island. Furthermore, all graves on the island were opened and their contents moved to a common grave on Rheneia, known as the 'purification pit'.

This second purification of Delos was followed by a new period of prosperity. The old festival was changed and alongside this annual celebration another one, held every five years, was inaugurated and a new major temple was erected. After the Spartan victory at the end of the Peloponnesian War in 403 BC, the Athenians temporarily lost their control over Delos, but Athenian general Conon recovered it again in 394 BC.

Athenian control of Delos lasted throughout the 4th century BC, despite the Delians' petition to the Delphic Oracle in an attempt to rid themselves of the Athenians in 345 BC. Athenian naval power began to wane at the end of the 4th century BC and the leadership of the Greek city-states passed to the Macedonians. Antigonos and his son Demetrios Poliorcetes formed an island confederation with Delos as its religious centre. The island was proclaimed free and independent in 314 BC. From then until 166 BC, Delos experienced a new period of prosperity, a period of Delian independence, which was not, however, absolute. The island was independent in name and governed by local rulers (the Hieropioi), who succeeded the Athenian amphictions and managed the sanctuary and its finances. But, in fact, it was under the Ptolemaic dynasty's sphere of influence, which also had general control over the Island Confederation. One of their concerns was the cultivation of good relations with the wealthy state of Rhodes, which resulted in a hindering of Delos' economic development. The Island Confederation was dissolved in 250 BC and the sacred island came, once again, under Macedonian influence. If, during the previous period, Delos benefited from competition among various rulers to offer

7

General view of the archaeological site of Delos from the SE with Rheneia in the background.

the greatest number of gifts and monuments to Apollo, under the Macedonians it was gradually transformed into a commercial centre of even greater importance. Characteristic of this commercial activity was the development of both private and public banks. Already by the second half of the 6th century BC, Delos had its own coinage, perhaps established during the Athenian Peisistratides' control and under the influence of Athenian coinage. During the Archaic period, in the 6th century BC, coins were silver in two drachmas, drachmas and smaller denominations. Later, they were bronze, all bearing the apollonian lyre, the symbol they retained until the

end, i.e. 167 BC, when the Athenians once again became masters of the island and withdrew all non-Athenian coinage. The important thing about the exchange of coins on Delos, was that, because of the multicultural population influx to the island, particularly in later years, coins from various cities were in circulation, a fact of great historical interest because its study can offer great insight into trade not only on Delos but throughout the Aegean. A large number of coins found on Delos come from the so-called "hoards" - large numbers of coins collected and hidden. Over thirty such hoards have been revealed at several locations, mainly in houses.

It is not certain if these were hidden at times of enemy incursions, as not everyone would have deposited their money in the banks. A hoard of this type was discovered in the House of the Comedians together with jewelry.

From the middle of the 3rd century and the beginning of the 2nd century BC, the port of Delos opened up to large-scale trade. Its natural geographical position placed it at the centre of the Mediterranean. It was thus used as one of the main hubs for the grain trade and the trafficking of other commercial goods between Numidia in North Africa and Chersonesos in the Crimea, but also West Asia, Syria and Egypt. The historian Strabo (X, 5, 4) informs us that Delos was also an important centre for the slave trade.

The ancient sacred character of the island dissipated in the cosmopolitan atmosphere that dominated the Macedonian port. New religions and new gods made their appearance – cautiously at first – before enjoying widespread popularity. The numbers of houses increased and more and more foreigners came to settle on the island. The local sanctuary officials tried to retain friendly relations with all. At the beginning of the 2nd century BC, however, Rome began to show its strength and in 168 BC the last King of Macedonia, Perseus, was defeated at Pydna. With the collapse of Macedonian power, Delos lost its powerful protectors and in 166 BC fell once more under the rule of the Athenians, to whom the victorious Romans offered the island, who declared Delos a free port in order to gain an advantage over the increasingly thriving Rhodes.

This second period of Athenian control began with the permanent expulsion of the Delians, who found refuge in Achaia from where they continued to protest against the Athenian occupation until they vanished permanently. It is possible that some Delians returned to their island later, but from this time on Delos was essentially an Athenian colony under the direct control of Rome.

At first, Delos was populated mainly by poor Athenians given a plot of land (cleruchs), as well as others with citizen status (astoi), who settled there and worked as clerics or merchants. Gradually, however, the demographic composition of the population changed, as amazingly successful economic growth also brought about a population increase. In the second half of the 2nd century and the beginning of the 1st century BC, there may have been 25,000 inhabitants. The Athenian element diminished then and gave way to other nationalities that came to settle at this rich port: Greeks from other city-states, Italians, Egyptians, Syrians, Phoenicians, Palestinians, and Jews. As a result, many, mainly eastern, cults flourished on Delos.

The Romans, true masters of the island, continued to control the Athenian administration, represented by the 'epimeletes' of Delos, appointed and dispatched every year from Athens.

The fact that Delos was dependent on, and closely linked to Rome, brought about the destruction of this great emporium and sanctuary. Mithridates Eupator, King of Pontus, in an attempt to strike his great enemies the Romans, attacked the flourishing Roman colony on Delos in 88 BC. Delos, unlike Athens, which was an ally of Mithridates, had sided with the Romans. The destruction that followed must have been nearly complete, although historical evidence presented by Appian and Pausanias, who suggest a death toll of 20,000, must be considered somewhat exaggerated. The Romans, however, reinstated Athenian control after their final

Partial view of the archaeological site of Delos from the SE.

victory and Sulla's visit to the island. The wars of Mithridates continued and, in 69 BC, the pirates of Athenodoros, an ally of Mithridates, destroyed all that remained and Delos lost both its commercial and sacred status.

When, almost immediately afterwards, the Romans once again became masters of the island and realized that the place's sanctity alone did not provide sufficient protection, they decided to wall the most important part of the town, i.e. the sanctuary and the theatre district. The Roman general Triarius carried out repair work wherever he could, and organized the hasty construction of a wall built of every kind of material available.

The Athenians retained control of the island whose sanctity was recognized by a decision of the Roman senate in 58 BC, which also conferred special privileges to its population. Life on Delos had, however, lost its previous luster. Its opulent houses were abandoned and most were turned into workshops, as recent excavations have shown. Moreover, the Athenians began to lose interest in Delos, as ports in Italy and the East took the place of this sacred island in Mediterranean commerce. Athens ceased to send an archon (governor) and appointed instead a lifelong priest of Apollo who, however, resided in Athens. An attempt to revive the old Delian festival, which had ceased in 316 BC, made by the philhellene Roman emperor Hadrian in the 2nd century AD, failed, and the twelve animals taken annually to Delos for sacrifice did not suffice to recreate the sacred atmosphere and awe of the ancient rituals. The Athenians became so disinterested in Delos that they put the island up for sale a short time later. There were no buyers.

The diminishment in area of the once massive settlement reduced the boundaries of Delos during the early Christian period (2nd-5th century AD) to the area between the Lesche of Poseidoniasts to the north and the lower part of the theatre quarter to the south, in other words on top of the ruins of the once powerful sacred shrine. By the end of the 3rd century AD, there was a small Christian settlement here; it is mentioned as a bishopric, an honour possibly conferred because of the island's earlier renown. The nearby islands of Mykonos, Syros, Kythnos and Kea came under its jurisdiction. Many small early Christian basilicas were constructed on Delos due to the plentiful building materials from the ancient ruins, which could be easily converted for Christian use. It has even been suggested that a monastery occupied the site of the famous Hypostyle Hall.

Neither, however, its status as the seat of a Bishopric, nor other external factors sufficed to restore Delos to its former status as a sacred and commercial centre. Indeed, they rather stressed the desolation that had overtaken it to such an extent that maps at the end of the 5th century AD called the island A-delos not Delos.

No signs of life were noted on Delos after the 6th century AD. After the 8th century AD it was not even mentioned in the Episcopal lists of the islands that belonged to the new bishopric of Syros.

In AD 727 it was pillaged by the troops of the iconoclast emperor Leo the Isaurian; again by the Slavs in 763, and in 821 by the Cretan Saracens. It may have also suffered Arab incursions. Destroyed and deserted it passed into Venetian hands but the Republic, having no use for it, gave it to a feudal lord of Mykonos. In AD 1329, a group of the Knights of St. John of Malta settled on the island for a short time. Both Delos and its scarcely populated neighbouring islands, after their occupation by the Turks in AD 1566, became pirate bases throughout the period of Ottoman occupation. This is when it became an important site for supplying building materials and for making lime from the large quantities of marble scattered about the island. The bronze clamps that once held the ancient buildings together were also very useful during the middle ages when metal was in short supply.

Delos, together with the neighbouring island of Rheneia, whose ancient name was forgotten, became known as Deles, a name that survives to this day (Mikres Deles or Delos and Megales Deles or Rheneia). Delos fell under the auspices of the Municipality of Mykonos, which leased land for pasture and cultivation to the few shepherds who inhabited the islands.

Delos remained unknown to the West until the Renaissance. The Arab geographer Edrisi (AD 1154), mentions it as Ardilo, a "round, deserted island with no inhabitants but a harbour". It is also mentioned on Italian portolans after the 13th century AD.

In AD 1445, Cyril of Ancona visited Mykonos and Delos where he was impressed by the roundness of the sacred lake which he describes as "a round naumachia, half a stadium wide" (referring to the naumachia in which Romans staged mock naval battles) and by the colossal statue of Apollo of the Naxians, which despite its mutilation dominated the entire site and was thus a common subject of travellers' sketches.

Greek and French archaeological excavations began on the island in 1872. The

General view of the Sanctuary of Apollo from the NW with Mt. Cynthus in the background.

Greek Archaeological Service was among the first Services of the newly formed Greek State. From 1873, however, the French School at Athens took over the systematic excavations that continue to this day, and brought to light, mainly from 1902-1914, the sanctuary of Apollo and a large part of the Hellenistic town. Since 1960, the Greek Archaeological Service has conserved mosaic floors and painted wall plaster, and has replaced architectural members to their original locations while restoring some of the buildings. It has also undertaken excavations on Rheneia (the necropolis, part of which is also being excavated by French archaeologists, the shrine of Hercules, and others – see p. 74), and on Delos periodically, i.e. during digging to lay electrical cables etc. Despite the fact that the excavated monuments are only a distant memory of the magnificence of "sacred Delos", the visitor cannot but be impressed by what he sees.

MONUMENTS*

For the visitor to gain full benefit from his visit it is advisable to divide the site into its separate parts, many of which offer an entirely different impression of the site as a whole. Areas such as the sanctuary, residential districts, the commercial centre, the sanctuaries dedicated to foreign gods, etc. are best appreciated as separate parts of the whole. It is probably superfluous to note that the three hours allowed by the boat schedule on Delos are not enough to even appreciate the quality of light in this unique place. The hurried visitor should allot at least two days exploration, while a full week would provide a relatively satisfactory insight.

The Sanctuary Area

Because Delos' fame and wealth derived from the presence of Apollo, the city surrounded the sanctuary, which occupies the centre of the low valley near the harbour.

Today's visitor, like his ancient counterpart, disembarks on the northwestern shore of the island, at the site of the ancient harbour (1), situated in a well-sheltered bay. The ancient harbour, known as the "sacred harbour" – much further south there was also a commercial harbour in front of the commercial district (see p. 67) – had a quay to the north in front of the so-called Agora of Theophrastos, while on its south side was the Agora of the Compitaliasts. This is the present entrance to the site, as the boats dock beside a strip of land created by the spoil heaps of the archaeological excavations. This Agora, known either as the Agora of the Hermaists, or of the Compitaliasts (2) – also referred to as Apolloniasts and Poseidoniasts on votive inscriptions – was constructed in the late Hellenistic period, mainly by merchants from Italy who had organized themselves into guilds under the protection of a particular god. It is an open square around which the guilds had settled, placing altars and small temples as well as shops and some temporary structures at its centre. The Compitaliasts were a combination of Roman free men and slaves who invoked the protection of the Lares of the crossroads (Compita).

The ancient road that led east and then north (3) is flanked by two large buildings, the Stoa (Portico) of Philip (4) on the left and the South Stoa (Portico) (5) on the right. The South Portico, 66 m long and 13 m wide, with 28 Doric columns along its façade, was built in the 3rd century BC by the Kings of Pergamon. At the Stoa's far side is a series of rooms used as shops. Opposite the South Stoa, Philip V of Macedonia dedicated another stoa, 72 m long and 11 m wide with 16 Doric columns situated between pilasters, to Apollo in 210 BC. The upper part of the walls of its short sides contained four windows each. The epistyle bore large letters, which read: *"The King of the Macedonians Philip, son of King Demetrios dedicates this to Apollo"*. Since this stoa had no direct access to the sea because its back wall

---

* The numbers in brackets refer to the general plan at the end of the book.

Above: The square of the Hermaists or Compitaliasts from the SE with the harbour in the background on the right.
Below: The Sacred Way from the S. On the left the Portico of Philip.

was closed off, another stoa, 15 m longer, whose façade opened out towards the harbour, was later added along the northern side. The gap created along the northern extension of the Portico (Stoa) of Philip was filled by a smaller chamber separated from the newer stoa by four elliptical columns. The newer western stoa was used for commercial purposes while its extension to the north was used, after 166 BC, as offices for the supervisors of trade. Between the two stoas, the Southern and the Stoa of Philip, stood a large number of statues, although only their bases or pedestals survive. Some of these appear to have been podium shaped (e.g. the offering of Sotelos, to the right of the Propylaea).

To the east of the Southern Stoa and virtually adjoining it, is a rectangular agora known as the Agora of the Delians, or Square Agora (**6**). It is a trapezium-shaped square with stoas along three sides. Statues on plinths and podiums stood in the square, while a narrow corridor led through the Southern Stoa to the Sacred Way. The single stoa along the south side was built in the 3rd century BC, while the other, L-shaped one, which forms the eastern and northern sides, was added in the 2nd century BC. The stoa's interior housed shops from an earlier period. The offices of the 'agoranomoi' (market officials) were on its second floor, which was supported by pillars rather than columns. In the 2nd century AD, the Romans built public baths in the centre of the square, of which survives the white mosaic floor of a large chamber.

The Sanctuary of Apollo

The main entrance to the sanctuary of Apollo was always from the south. There, the Athenians, around the middle of the 2nd century BC, built the Propylaea (**7**), which survive to this day, replacing an earlier gateway. The marble entrance with Doric columns in front and behind stands on a platform with three steps. After climbing the steps, the visitor has to his right the stele of Hermes Propylaios, erected by the Amphictions in 342/1 BC. Continuing along the Sacred Way, on the right is the main sanctuary of Apollo, while on the left are other buildings, of which the most important is the Artemision, the sanctuary of Artemis, Apollo's sister.

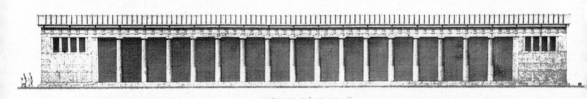

Reconstruction of the Portico (Stoa) of Philip (G. Poulsen, 1911).

The Propylaea with Hermes Propylaeos. On the right the Oikos of the Naxians.

Beginning with the Temple of Apollo, the first building on the right, almost abutting the Propylaea is the Oikos of the Naxians (**8**) (for the Oikos building type, see p. 19). This is one of the buildings the Naxians dedicated to Apollo; it dates from the 7th century BC, or possibly earlier. Based on the evidence brought to light by the excavations at the beginning of the 20th century AD, it was thought there was a first building phase, known as "pre-Oikos", with two rows of wooden columns within a long and narrow building constructed in the second half of the 7th century BC. This theory, based on the deep incisions in the soft rock for the placement of the wooden internal columns is no longer accepted. The first building phase therefore, around the first quarter of the 6th century BC, produced the structure roughly in the form it survives to this day - a long and narrow building with a single row of columns down its long axis. In its first phase, it was built of large granite blocks with a simple entrance roughly half way along its northern side. The main entrance to the west comprised two columns in antis creating an antechamber. In the sekos were eight delicate Ionic columns each placed on a drum on a circular base. A marble floor and a prostoon with four columns were added on the east side during the second half of the 6th century BC. The roof was made entirely of Naxian marble, a great technical achievement, whose creator is recorded as the Naxian Byzis who, according to Pausanias, invented the marble tile. The building also had gorgons carved on the antefixes. The use of the Oikos of the Naxians has baffled scholars. Some suppose that this was the first temple of Apollo; others offered different explanations. Today it is considered, always with

17

Above: The Colossus of the Naxians in two parts, as it is today in the NW corner of the Artemision. Below: Drawing of the ruins on Delos by the traveller Seger de Vries (1673). In front, the colossal statue of the Naxians.

some uncertainty, to have been a building used for gatherings and symposiums. Along the northern wall the Naxians erected a colossal statue of Apollo as a kouros, i.e. a naked youth in frontal position with his left leg forward and his arms pressed against the body, with a slight bend at the elbows and fists clenched. This statue of Apollo was roughly four times larger than life-size (approximately 9 m high), and stood on a hexagonal base (**9**), on the eastern side of which an inscription reads: "I am of the same piece of marble, both statue and base". The inscription on the western side of the base, which reads "the Naxians to Apollo", was probably added in the 4th century BC when the statue was reinstated after being toppled by the falling bronze Palm Tree of Nicias. Only the base, broken into several pieces, survives in its initial position next to the north wall of the Oikos of the Naxians. Several attempts to move it were made during various more recent periods of pillaging, but it remained on the island because of its massive weight. Its main body was cut in half for greater ease in moving. It is now located in the western corner of the Artemision in two pieces, missing its head and extremities. It must have been a kouros with arms away from the body, probably holding a bow in one hand and an arrow or flask in the other. It would also have had additional metal parts such as long curls on the head and a belt around the waist. It dates from 600 to 560 BC.

Approximately 6 m east of the Oikos of the Naxians survive the foundations of a rectangular building that measures 3.55 x 7.95 m and is aligned north-south with an entrance from the north (megaron C) (10). This was thought once to be an older temple of Apollo; a theory no longer accepted.

The last building in this area, to the south of the Oikos of the Naxians, is divided into three parts, identified as the Workshops of the Theandridon (11), one of the old tritties (tribes) of Delos. The fyles, tritties and fratries were the social groups to which the town's men belonged.

The Sacred Way, lined with the bases of votive statues on both sides, opens out in front of the pedestal of the Colossus of the Naxians. To the right is an 8 m long base made of deep blue marble with a large dedicatory inscription. Known as the base of Philetairos, founder of the Pergamon dynasty, it was erected in his honour after his death in the second half of the 3rd century BC to support statues of himself and members of his dynasty.

Behind this base are the ruins of the three temples of Apollo. The northernmost is known as the Porinos Naos (12) and was built by the Athenians in the third quarter of the 6th century BC. It is named for the porous limestone that the Athenians used in its construction. Unfortunately only its foundations, which form a rectangle divided in two parts, survive. It appears that the temple was prostyle, i.e. apart from a sekos it also had a vestibule on its western side where the entrance with six Ionic columns was situated. The Athenians also built the adjacent temple after the purification of 425 BC. Built of Pentelic marble in honour of Apollo, the Athenian general Nicias inaugurated it during the Quinquennial Theoria festival of 417 BC. It measured 17 x 11 m, was constructed in the Doric order, and was amphiprostyle, i.e. each narrow end had six columns that rested on a high raised base with four steps and the prodomos had four square pillars between the antae. A wall separated the sekos from the prodomos and there were two windows on either side of the entrance. Within the sekos was a semicircular base of blue-green Eleusinian marble upon which stood seven statues (of which one must have been that of Apollo). The temple was thus known as the Oikos of the Seven (13). Some of the sculptural decoration from the acroteria, now housed in the Delos Museum, has survived. The best-known piece is from the eastern pediment and depicts Boreas abducting Oreithyia. A second group, depicting Eos abducting Cephalos from an acroterion of the west pediment survives but is severely fragmented.

The third and largest temple, known as the Temple of the Delians (14), dominated

Reconstruction of the Sanctuary at the beginning of the 1st century BC (Ph. Fraisse – M.-Ch. Hellmann – Y. Rizakis, 1966).

the sanctuary. Its construction began with the establishment of the Athenian League in 478 BC. It is the only peripteral temple on Delos, with six Doric columns along its narrow and thirteen along its long sides. The entrance is situated on the west side and the interior construction consists of a pronaos, single-aisled sekos and an opisthodomos with two columns in antis. Construction stopped, however, with the transferal of the League's treasury from Delos to Athens in the mid 5th century BC. The Delians completed the temple by the end of the 4th century BC, without, however, managing to put the finishing touches to the architectural decoration.

Returning to the Sacred Way and heading north, one comes on the right to a small paved square, around which are the ruins of a Mycenaean settlement (**15**) (1400-1200 BC), which extend to the east under the Artemision and to the south under the Porinos Naos and the temple of the Athenians. Ruins of other Mycenaean houses survive under Stoa D of the Artemision, under the Pythion and, mainly under temple G. In addition, part of a wall in the northeastern corner of the temple of Apollo is thought to belong to the Mycenaean settlement's boundaries. Characteristic of these houses is that their entrances are generally near the corners and are usually large and monolithic.

Heading north the visitor comes to the first of five Oikoi or Treasuries (**16-19a**) arranged in an arc behind the three temples of Apollo from north to northeast. This type of building, shaped like a small temple, was constructed by city-states to house their portable offerings to the god. Some may have been used as eating

Reconstruction of the façade of the Great Temple of Apollo (F. Courby, G. Poulsen, 1931).

Reconstruction of the façade of the temple of the Athenians.

21

Reconstruction of the Porinos Naos or Oikos (F. Courby – G. Poulsen, 1931).

places or rest houses for pilgrims. The westernmost of these (**16**) was erected by the Carystians in the 6th century BC. It had a prostoon with four columns and an interior colonnade along the length of the sekos. The columns may have been in the Doric order.

The other four temples were built in the first half of the next century following the same architectural plan as the first. The second in line (**17**) was larger than the rest, and was divided into two sections by three pillars. In the prodomos there would have been four or five columns in antis. The fourth (**18**) was possibly the Estiatorion of the Keans mentioned by Herodotus; it had two columns in antis, as did the other treasuries (**19-19a**).

Slightly to the east of the treasuries survive the ruins of a long and narrow building, known as building D (**20**). This is thought to be the Bouleuterion, founded in the first half of the 6th century BC. An interior colonnade divides the larger southern area, with two entrances on the west side, into two wings. A dedicatory column bearing an inscription to Athena Polias, which also dates from the 6th century BC, stand at the outside northeastern corner.

Next to building D, was the Prytaneion (**21**), partially built in the first half of the 5th century and completed in the 4th century BC. It is a composite building divided laterally into three sections with the entrance on the south side. There were four Doric columns in the prodomos and marble benches against the walls. The middle section was an internal marble-paved courtyard. The third and largest section was subdivided into two rectangular halls, each with its own prodomos. Within the prodomos of the western hall were two very small rooms on the right, which, after 166 BC, housed the cult of the Demos (city) of Athens and Rome. In the main hall, where the Prytaneis met, the foundations of the altar of Hestia can still be seen. The eastern hall may have been used as a restroom. Two small recesses in the northern side seem to have been used as the repository of the town's archives. Above the

Reconstruction of the Prytaneion (H. Lauter, 1968).

entrance colonnade there seems to have been a kind of loggia running the length of the façade.

West of the Prytaneion are five altars, of which three are Archaic, one is Classical, and one is Hellenistic. One of the Archaic altars was dedicated to Zeus Polieus and Athena Polias; the Classical one to Athena and Apollo Paiona. This area of altars, dedicated to urban deity-guardians (– *poliades*), were not part of the sanctuary, as a wall separated them from it.

East of building D and the Prytaneion, and parallel to them, stood one of the most distinctive structures of Greek antiquity, a long and narrow building conventionally called the Monument of the Bulls (**22**). It is identified today as the Neorion, mentioned in inscriptions. It is 69.40 m long and 10.37 m wide and had pilasters, possibly with railings between them, in the walls of the long sides. The building was divided into three sections: the prodomos on the south side with a prostasis of six Doric columns and two more along the sides, the central, longest section with marble floor, benches along the sides, and painted decoration low on the walls, and the northern compartment where a large triangular built base survives. The middle and northern sections communicate via three openings between two unusual supports formed by half-columns on one side and pilasters on the other; the latter crowned by two bulls' heads facing one another. In the northern section, the roof is higher than over the rest of the building and the Ionic pillars that supported the central section formed openings. This building's unusual shape seems to have been due to the fact that it was built to house a trireme, possibly dedicated by Demetrios Poliorcetes after a naval victory. In this case, this section of the building can be identified as the Neorion mentioned in inscriptions. It is possible that the northern compartment was initially used for religious ceremonies because the openings in the raised roof have led to the assumption that an altar with an eternal flame may have existed here. The monument of the Bulls, inaugurated towards the end of the 4th century BC, was the first of the series of buildings erected in the sanctuary of Apollo by rulers of the Hellenistic period.

A few meters to the southeast, the marble base of the altar of Zeus Soter and

The Portico of Antigonos from the E with the statue of Gaius Billienus in front.

Athena Soteira, originally built at the beginning of the 3rd century BC, has been reconstructed (**23**). East of the altar and heading north is a well-preserved section of the sanctuary's Hellenistic boundary wall (**24**). Built of rows of gneiss alternating with granite, it enclosed the sanctuary to the east. At the northernmost edge, three exedrae (**25**) were used as bases for statues of private individuals, beyond which stood the statue of Gaius Billienus (**26**) a Roman ruler depicted as general (end of the 2nd – beginning of the 1st century BC).

The north side of the sanctuary was enclosed by a large, long, and narrow stoa built after the middle of the 3rd century BC by the King of Macedonia, Antigonos Gonatas, as stated in the fragmented votive inscription above the entablature: "King Antigonos of Macedon son of King Demetrios to Apollo". The Portico (Stoa) of Antigonos (**27**), 119 m long and 20 m wide, is Π-shaped with its two sides running southward. The façade's colonnade comprised 47 Doric columns made of blue-grey Tenos marble, fluted only on the upper parts. Every second triglyph bears a carved and painted marble bull's head. There was a second Ionic colonnade on the interior. This stoa was purely votive, not commercial. The entire area in front of it was full of votive offerings: approximately 60 statues, bases, exedrae, etc, while on the rectangular base to the north stood approximately 20 bronze statues of Antigonos' ancestors (**28**).

Roughly halfway along the stoa is the Theke of Opis and Arge (**29**). This is one of two Mycenaean tombs linked in ancient historic times to the worship of the mythical Hyperborean Virgins who came to help Leto during Apollo's birth and remained on Delos as priestesses. Today, the Theke is a semi-circular exedra that

The Minoa Fountain from the SE.

determines the abaton (a place whose entrance is forbidden), within which the tomb stands. The latter consists of a built rectangular chamber approached by a dromos (road).

Outside the Stoa of Antigonos, on the northern side of the sanctuary, is the Minoa Fountain (**30**), built during the second half of the 6th century BC and well known from inscriptions. Excavated in the granite to a depth of more than 4 m, it contained water all year round and is almost square (4 x 3.75 m). Along three sides it had walls built of gneiss while on the fourth was a staircase with eleven steps that led down to the water. Above the cistern was a built structure, a kind of covered enclosure that left space for a corridor along three sides. On the side of the entrance, i.e. the south side, was a stoa with six columns in the front and two more at the sides. A 4th century BC inscription lists the fines imposed on anyone who washed anything, including themselves, or threw anything into the water.

Next to the Stoa of Antigonos to the west there is a carefully built rectangular marble building. This construction, identified in inscriptions as "Graphe" or "Oikos" (**31**), was initially thought to serve a public (administrative) function. According to more recent theories, however, it was probably used to store paintings. It was probably built at the end of the 5th or the beginning of the 4th century BC, and a small Doric stoa was added to the south side during a later building phase in the 3rd century BC.

Returning to the Propylaea, the visitor proceeds to the western section of the sanctuary. Opposite the Oikos of the Naxians, to the left of the Propylaea, stood the Portico (Stoa) of the Naxians (**32**), a Γ-shaped building in the southwest corner of

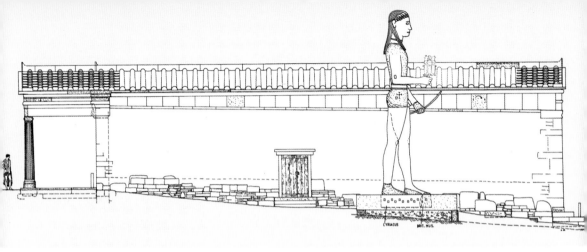

Reconstruction of the Oikos of the Naxians (G. Gruben, 1997).

the sanctuary built in the mid 6th century BC. The stoa's western wall was built on the promenade with a marble ledge running its length. In the stoa's interior, the colonnade had slender Ionic columns, ten on the south side and at least seventeen on the west side. The roof, like the Oikos of the Naxians, was built exclusively of Naxian marble.

Athenian general Nicias set a bronze palm tree (**33**) in the inside corner of the Stoa, probably when he came to Delos for the inauguration of the temple of the Athenians in 417 BC. The marble and granite base, which still bears Nicias' inscribed name, remains in its original position. As mentioned by Pausanias, the palm tree was blown down by a strong wind in antiquity and knocked over the Colossus of the Naxians. Continuing to the west, one comes to two almost identical buildings entered from the east that cannot be identified with particular monuments. The southern building, a simple single room, had a pyramid-shaped roof held up by four internal supports. It may have been used for symposiums and could be identified as the Oikos of the Andrians (**34**). The northern building, known as the Monument of the Hexagons (**35**), contains unusual examples of architectural decoration. The surface of the marble walls is covered with a honeycomb of continuous hexagons. This pattern, found on other monuments in the Aegean area – on Thasos, a colony of Paros, at Sani in Chalkidiki, a colony of Andros, at Erythres in Ionia, on Paros, but also at the Letoon on Delos (see p. 30) – is thought to be Cycladic in inspiration. The building had a roof similar to the previous building and, apart from the door, must have had three windows and openings, an unusual architectural element that can, however, be explained by the building's use, perhaps a restaurant, or for an altar. Researchers have suggested that it may have been used as a Hieropieion (meeting place of the Hieropioi), Oikos of the Parians, or that of the Delians. It may have been built around 500 BC.

In the area in front of the Stoa of the Naxians and to the east is the Pillar of Antiochos, upon which stood the statue of Antiochos III, King of Syria (223-187 BC), as the inscription on its northern side states. The pillar, made of blue-grey marble, has been reconstructed to a height of approximately 25 m.

Further north, among the ruins of various monuments, some of which belong to the Mycenaean period, noteworthy is the tomb of two more Hyperborean Virgins, namely the Sema of Laodice and Hyperoche (**36**), of which only a small section of the

26

semi-circular wall survives and can thus only be identified by Herodotus's reference that the "Sema" was located on the left side of the entrance to the Artemision.

Immediately north of the Pillar of Antiochos are the ruins of an arched construction known as the "Arched building" (37), which is identified as the Keraton mentioned in inscriptions. Despite the poor preservation of its architectural remains, their study has resulted in the artist's reconstruction of a monumental altar on a raised base that was arched in the east and open in the west and possibly had a sloping floor with stairs along both sides. The area from the Propylaea to the Oikos of the Naxians in front of the altar was paved with blue-grey marble plaques. It is widely accepted that this is the famous "Keratinos altar" built by Apollo himself; also identifiable as the "great altar", which Kallimachos mentions in his *Ode to Delos*. Apart from its use as an altar, however, the "Arched building" must also have housed, in its arched section, a holy relic protected by a type of canopy (removable cover). The western open section was used for various ceremonies, including possibly cattle sacrifices, offerings to Apollo, and other rituals including flagellation, mentioned by various ancient sources, including Kallimachos, and the geranos, the crane dance first performed by Theseus on his return from Crete with the young Athenians he had saved from the Minotaur.

Immediately north of the Keraton altar one can just about make out the remains of a small temple, known as temple G (38), as it cannot be connected to a particular god. Its interior contains traces of a Mycenaean structure, known as "Mansion H". In front of the temple extends a paved area dating from the Hellenistic period, with Mycenaean remains beneath. Between the Keraton and the Artemision survive the foundations of a spacious, almost square, building divided into two sections, a sekos and a pronaos, with twelve Ionic columns along its façade. Its probable identification is the Pytheion (39) mentioned in inscriptions that tell us that its internal chamber, which had an opening in the roof, housed a bronze palm tree and three statues. There was also a Π-shaped interior colonnade, and an eternal fire from which the Lemnians and others came every year to renew their city's hestia (hearth). The Athenians built it around the middle of the 4th century BC.

The visitor now finds himself at the boundaries of the sanctuary of Artemis, Apollo's sister, which extended over the northwestern area of the sanctuary (40). Archaeological excavations revealed a Mycenaean building thought to have been the first temple of Artemis, but this is now doubtful. The building was unusually long (approximately 15.30 m) with an entrance at the eastern edge of the long south side, outside of which a deposit of Mycenaean chryselephantine objects was discovered. Most of these were flat tiles with relief representations used to decorate furniture or boxes, possibly from tombs, although some may have been waste material from workshops. The best known of these bears the representation of a warrior; others depict animals struggling with imaginary beasts.

The Mycenaean temple was replaced by a second one, relatively large for its time, at the beginning of the 7th century BC, or perhaps a little later. Built diligently out of thin gneiss plaques, its sekos measured 8.60 x 9.60 m. Votive statues of kores (young females finely dressed), now housed in the Delos Museum, stood around the temple until the end of the 6th century BC. There was also a seventh century BC female statue in the form of a 'xoanon' (idol) dedicated by the Naxian

Nikandra, now in the National Archaeological Museum in Athens. It is the oldest monumental sculpture to have survived from Archaic Greece.

The third and final temple of Artemis was built during the period of Delian independence (314-116 BC), after the peripteral temple of Apollo. It was prostyle, with six Ionic columns along its façade (the east side). A Γ-shaped portico, preserved in its 2nd century BC form, enclosed the temple of Artemis to the east and north while on its west side there were three more columns made of blue-grey marble, which belonged to a Stoa built during the Athenians' second rule over Delos that faced the sea.

From the beginning of the 5th century BC, the northwestern corner of the sanctuary of Apollo was enclosed by two buildings. One, with a fairly complicated floor plan, is known as the "building with the colonnaded court" (**41**). It was once thought to be a Thesmophorion but, is now widely thought to have functioned as a restaurant. It is a long and narrow building divided into three sections: two identical rooms with a roof supported by four central Ionic columns and, between these two rooms, a colonnaded courtyard. The columns were made of limestone with marble capitals and had painted decoration. Adjacent to this building was the Ecclesiasterion (**42**), built to house the meeting of the Ecclesia, i.e. the city council. Its present form of two adjacent halls was created after numerous alterations and additions from the 5th to the 2nd centuries BC. The uppermost section of the walls in the larger western room contained openings divided by rectangular pilasters and its south side formed an apse. Along the room's sides were marble benches. Deep inside, to the north, a small marble temple with two columns in antis was erected in the Roman period, probably to house a statue. During the early Christian period, a basilica was constructed on the ruins of these two buildings.

The area west and north of the Sanctuary

Leaving the sanctuary at its northwest corner the visitor comes to a large expanse, usually covered by water, known as the Agora of Theophrastos (**43**). Theophrastos was the 'epimeletes' of the Athenians on Delos in 126/5 BC, when this area was created. At the square's northwestern corner survives a tall blue marble base with an inscribed plinth of white marble, upon which the statue of Theophrastos stood, as the inscription relates.

To the north there was a building from the 3rd century BC known as the Hypostyle Hall (**44**). Delian inscriptions from the small sanctuary of Poseidon Nauklarios to the south of the building refer to it as the Portico (Stoa) of Poseidon. The hall is a large rectangular room, measuring 56.45 x 34.30 m, open only along its south side at the entrance. 44 columns in nine rows supported the roof and 15 Doric columns between pilasters formed the façade. The inscription on the architrave reads "the Delians offered this to Apollo" (after 166 BC the word "Athenians" replaced the word "Delians"). The columns along the length of the side walls were Doric while the rest were Ionic. A kind of skylight was formed above the gap created by the empty space in the centre. The building belongs to an architectural type rare in Greece and may have been a place for meeting and

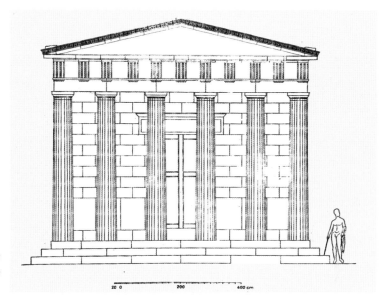

*Reconstruction
of the façade
of the Dodecatheon.*

20 0   200   400 cm

strolling. This area is also one of the few locations in Delos where early Christian remains are visible; e.g. above the ruins of the Hypostyle Hall survive structures dating from the 4th and 5th century AD.

A few meters further north are the ruins of the Dodecatheon (**45**), a temple dedicated to the twelve gods that dates from the Archaic period. In its initial form it must have included one or more altars and statues, many of which have survived in fragments. Many altars continued to be built throughout the 4th century BC, particularly in the area between the temple and the Agora of the Italians. At the beginning of the Hellenistic period (end of the 4th, beginning of the 3rd century BC), an amphiprostyle hexastyle temple was also erected with six columns along its two narrow sides.

To the left of the Dodecatheon towers the grey bulk of the so-called Granite Monument (**46**), a large building complex constructed of granite, which covered an area of 40 x 19.50 m and contained around 15 shops; many fragments of flutes and other objects connected to their manufacture were found in roughly one quarter of these, which may thus without doubt be identified as musical instrument workshops. The complex, entered from the south, had ground and first floors. It dates from the second half of the 2nd century BC and may have served as a meeting place for religious associations.

On the other side of the road that led to the northern part of the archaeological site is the Letoon (**47**), a temple dedicated to Apollo's mother, Leto. It was built after the middle of the 6th century BC, approximately 540 BC, and faces south toward the Sanctuary of Apollo. It consists of a pronaos, which may have been unroofed, with an entrance to the west and a wide sekos. Between the pronaos and the sekos is a wide entrance with two columns in antis. A marble bench runs the length of the

The Letoon from the SW.

exterior of the temple walls, whose upper parts were of slate. In the middle of the sekos survive the foundations of the base of the statue of Leto, who was depicted seated, while around the walls is a low ledge, used for the placing offerings. The Letoon is the only Archaic temple outside the sanctuary of Apollo and Artemis, and it seems that the area over which Leto had jurisdiction was very large: to the north and east over the entire area later occupied by the Agora of the Italians. The geographer Strabo (63 BC-26 AD) refers to the Letoon as the entire area of the town north of the sanctuary of Apollo. This in itself testifies the importance of the worship of Leto (a prehistoric deity) in the Archaic period.

East of the Letoon and adjacent to it was a large agora, known as the Agora of the Italians (**48**), built at the end of the 2nd century BC. It extends over an area measuring 48 x 68 m and the entrance was through a propylon at its southwest corner. On each side of the rectangle formed by the various outbuildings was a colonnade; the resulting peristyle created a large uncovered area. Above this colonnade was a second one with square pilasters, so that the second floor rooms looked out over a balcony, which ran along all four sides. At ground level, exedras or loggias opened off the colonnade; these were relatively spacious and were sometimes subdivided into smaller spaces by columns. Shops entered from the road occupied two sides and there was a bath-house in the northeastern corner. The Agora was built mainly at the expense of rich sponsors, such as the banker Philostratos of Askalon in Phoenicia, who donated the northern Doric colonnade, and the rich merchant Gaius Ofellius Ferus of Champagne, who conducted business on Delos. The latter financed the construction of a stoa and placed a larger-than-life statue of himself in a niche. According to the inscription on its base this was the work of the Athenian sculptors Dionysius and Timarchides. This

Reconstruction of the niche with the statue of Gaius Ofellius Ferus (A. Stewart – C. H. Smith, 1990).

monumental complex, the biggest on Delos, became the meeting place for merchants from Italy and elsewhere, who had settled on the island, and is an example of the financial supremacy of the Italian community in Hellenistic Delos. Recently, several scholars have suggested that the Agora of the Italians was the main centre of the slave trade as, according to ancient historians, Delos was one of the most important centers in the Mediterranean for this type of commerce. It is more likely, however, that slave traders functioned throughout the area, particularly around the harbour where squares and open spaces were used for trading and trafficking all types of merchandise. It is thought that roughly 30,000 people lived on Delos at the beginning of the 1st century BC.

The road that passes next to the Letoon heading north leads to an area where at the end of the 7th century BC the Naxians erected a row of lions on a level terrace (**49**). There were probably at least nine and may have been as many as sixteen. Today, five survive on Delos and have been moved to the Museum; their places

The terrace of the lions from the SW.

taken by copies in 2000. The headless body of a sixth lion was removed to the Arsenal in Venice, where it was restored with the addition of a modern head. The lions are seated on their haunches and face east, their gaze fixed on the Sacred Lake (**50**) where Phoebus Apollo was born. The Sacred Lake was formed by a marsh along the lower reaches of the Inopos and, according to ancient literary sources, was circular. It was drained for sanitary reasons and a palm tree planted in its centre in 1925.

Northwest of the row of lions stand the restored columns of a large building identified as the Koinon of the Poseidoniasts of Beirut (**51**), which can only be seen from a distance. The merchants and ship-owners from Beirut, who comprised the Koinon of the Poseidoniasts, built it low on the hill that rises up toward the small northern cove of the island. A peristyle court opened out in front of the building, which contained a number of rooms that served various purposes – clubs, money exchange services, and hostel– along its south side. On the west side were four small sekoi used for the worship of Poseidon and a number of Syrian gods, but also the goddess Roma. It dates from the first half of the 2nd century BC.

The rest of the expanse to the north of the sanctuary, known as the Area of the Hill, Scardana, and the Lake, is covered by the remains of the ancient city that grew up around the sanctuary. Some, as we shall see further down, extended even further. The most important of these is the oldest – the Theatre quarter (see below p. 45) south of the sanctuary. The northern area is more recent and has a better urban plan. The roads are quite wide, reaching up to 5 m, laid-out at right angles on a north-south east-west axis. The area south of the Theatre, conversely, has

The columns of the Koinon of the Poseidoniasts.

narrower winding roads, which follow the contours of the rising ground. This difference in urban planning is due to two historical factors. In the old settlements to the south construction was haphazard, as in most old towns where anyone with a plot of land could build on it. In the area to the north, the population influx into the multicultural Hellenistic town was the reason behind the organization of a well-planned urban settlement to house these new inhabitants. The roads had properly covered drains and some, the most commercial, were paved; the rest comprised of trodden earth. The blind outer walls on many houses were covered with symbols used to ward off bad spirits and to protect the house and its inhabitants, to fend off, as we say, the evil eye. These symbols, carved into the marble, gneiss or granite included phalluses, some of which were winged (the phallus also symbolized fertility), the piloi (conical hats) of the Dioskouroi, and an object probably representing Hercules' club.

Leaving the Koinon of the Poseidoniasts and ascending along its southern side one follows a road that, at its southwestern corner turns north and meets another path, which served four large housing complexes that extend to the north. For the visitor who wants to explore every corner of the ancient town, this road becomes a rough path through an area left largely unexcavated. It ascends the western slope of the hill, at the top of which is the so-called House of the Hill (**52**), whose walls stand to a height of 4.50 m and whose rooms, symmetrically situated around a courtyard with a Doric peristyle, have many windows, most of which were narrow triangular openings. Opposite this house, a heavy rainfall revealed part of a richly painted façade on the entrance of a house that had not yet been excavated. These

Reconstruction of the interior of the House of the Hill (J. Chamonard – A. Gabriel, 1922).

important wall paintings – currently in the Museum – were executed on nine successive layers of mortar and represented subjects connected to the Compitaliasts, their festivals, their protector deities, etc.

Returning to the same path, the visitor finds himself at the northwestern corner of the Koinon of the Poseidoniasts where a right-angled turn leads to the aforementioned four large building complexes. The first on the left, known as the «Nisis» of the Bronzes (**53**), comprises many relatively small spaces, some of which are on different levels, with courtyards in between. To the west survives an oikos (reception hall), with mosaic floor, limestone pilasters, and a well in the courtyard with an Ionic structure built over it. A large number of bronze objects, mainly inlays from furniture, doors, etc., were discovered here together with many everyday utensils and vessels. A dozen moulds for casting *anaklindra* (couch) legs (exhibited in the Museum) were found in a nearby shop since Delos was famous in antiquity for its production of bronze objects, mainly *anaklindra* (couches) of a particular "Delian" type.

To the northwest of the «Nisis» is a house where an unexpected discovery was made: approximately 15,000 clay sealings, *rypoi*, to use their ancient name, were found in a layer of ashes caused by a fire which possibly destroyed the house; the *rypoi* were preserved accidentally because they were baked. These are small pieces of clay, 0.01 – 0.075 m long, mostly long and narrow, bearing one or more seal impressions (some bear up to twelve), which were used to seal papyri after these were tied with a type of thread (possibly linen). The *rypoi*, which had a hole through their vertical axis, were attached to the thread and helped secure the rolled-up papyrus. They were found on the first floor of the house, which must have been the office of a rich individual, possibly a banker. The representations on the *rypoi* (see below p. 124) are significant as they represent statue types only known from here and so are of great art historical value. At the same time they offer precise information on the religious and artistic trends of Delian society during the Hellenistic period. The seals that impressed them date from the second half of the

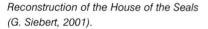
Reconstruction of the House of the Seals (G. Siebert, 2001).

Reconstruction of the roof of the House of the Sword (Fr. Alabe – N. Sigalas, 2002).

2nd and the beginning of the 1st centuries BC, but there are also some from the end of the 3rd century BC. The house was consequently named the House of the Seals (**54**). In a room on the ground floor a 3rd century BC millstone made of volcanic rock was discovered. It was named the "Delian mill" and is the oldest example of its type to survive from ancient Greece.

To the west of the House of the Seals is a courtyard belonging to another house, named the courtyard of the Sword (**55**), as a sword was discovered on the floor there together with fragments of a wonderful wall painting depicting floral decorations around a colonnade with Corinthian capitals.

Returning to the entry point on the road leading from north to east opposite the «Nisis» of the Bronzes is the so-called «Nisis» of the Jewels (**56**), where two groups of gold jewelry – necklaces, bracelets, earrings, etc (see below Museum) – and coins were found. There were also two mosaic floors: a small one depicting the mythological theme of Lycourgos and Ambrosia (probably from an upstairs room), and a larger one on the ground floor, representing Athena, Hermes and others; these are now in the Museum.

To the north of this block are the excavated remains of a building complex

The atrium of the House of the Comedians from the SE.

known as the «Nisis» of the House of the Comedians (**57**). This «Nisis» is formed by four houses built around 125 BC, which have a strange architectural design compared to other Delian houses. The westernmost of these, known as the House of the Pediments (**58**), had a two-storey tower, unique on Delos. The second is known as the House of the Comedians, because it contained a painted frieze, divided into metopes, most of which depict representations of actors in scenes from theatrical performances. The house's peristyle is unique in Delian private architecture. The Doric colonnade of the ground floor rose to the first floor Ionic wing and the entire structure reached a height of 9 m. The third, the House of the Tritons (**59**), east of the last, had a wonderful mosaic floor divided into two parts; one was lost in antiquity, but the other, which survives, represents a Tritonis (a sea nymph), holding a rudder while an Eros flies above her. It is thought that the missing part depicted a Triton, which, together with the Tritonis, would have comprised romantic couple. It dates from the 2nd century BC.

Exiting onto the road that descends along the north side of the Koinon of the Poseidoniasts, on the left, i.e. north of the road and east of the «Nisis» of the Jewels, is the house of the Diadoumenos (**60**), named thus because excavations revealed a 2nd century copy BC of the marvelous statue by Polykleitos depicting a youth, possibly Apollo, with arms raised to place a diadem on his head – today in the National Archaeological Museum in Athens. The building is very large (36 x 26 m) for a private house and for this reason many scholars believe it may have

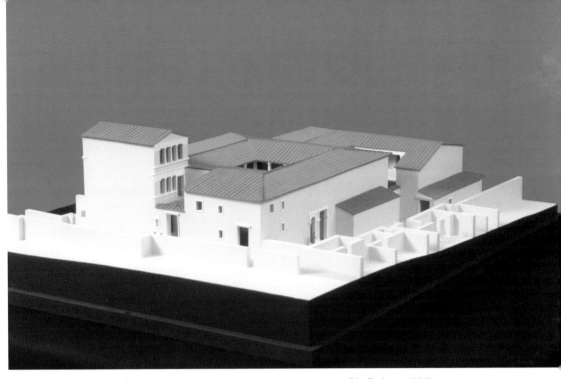

Reconstruction of the House of the Comedians complex (Ph. Bruneau – Ph. Fraisse, 1996).

▲ *Reconstruction of the atrium of the House of the Comedians
(Ph. Bruneau – P. Fister, 1970).*

▶ *Reconstruction of the wall with the frieze of the Comedians
(U. Bezerra de Meneses – Niels Bresch, 1970).*

The House with the Pediment
(Ph. Bruneau – Ph. Fraisse, 1970).

Mosaic floor representing a female Triton from the House of the Tritons.

functioned like the Koinon of the Poseidoniasts. It also had a very interesting plumbing system - a pipe filled a covered cistern with water that had already settled in another open cistern (the water was, in other words, already partially filtered), and there was a separate well housed in a rectangular room to the west of the first cistern. A tympanum with relief representations, a unique find at Delos and probably imported, survives in its original position.

Continuing to the east and on the right is a small complex with a triangular sanctuary at its southeastern corner. A few meters to the north is the so-called House of the Lake (**61**) with a beautiful peristyle whose blue-grey columns survive in situ.

The House of Diadoumenos is adjacent to two public buildings connected to athletic activities. To the northeast is the Palaestra of Granite, the Palaestra of the Lake is to the southeast. The first chronologically "older" or "ancient" palaestra is the so-called Palaestra of the Lake (**62**), and can possibly be identified as the Gymnasium mentioned in inscriptions as being re-constructed in approximately 130 BC before being abandoned in favour of the Gymnasium (see below p. 41), which was constructed at the beginning of the 1st century BC. The construction of this palaestra dates from the 3rd century BC and, despite its frequent refurbishing, its basic shape remained roughly the same – a variety of rooms along its four sides around a courtyard with a cistern in the middle. The second palaestra, known as the Palaestra of Granite (**63**), was built in the 2nd century BC and is a large four-sided building with an entrance to the west. It has an open square courtyard with an underground cistern in the centre. Stoas with granite columns enclose the

The Palaestra of Granite from the NW.

courtyard on all sides. On the north side, in accordance with the convention for gymnasiums, is a second colonnade, parallel to the exterior wall, while rooms open out from the other three sides; these include the Ephebeion, in the middle of the western side, a room open to the courtyard and used for rest and conversation. A marble bench ran around the walls and there were baths in the southwest corner.

On the east side, the palaestra's wall was incorporated into the wall of Triarius (**64**), built in 69 BC by the Roman governor Triarius to protect Delos from new incursions. The wall began at the bay of Scardanas, continued to the east and ended south of the Theatre quarter (see below p. 46). The visitor reaches its northwestern edge, the location of the so-called House of Scardanas (**65**), by ascending a few steps onto a plateau running along the western side of the Palaestra of Granite and reaching a part of the wall of Triarius. Another path on the left leads to the house, which is the northernmost in this area, built close to the small bay. Two columns survive in the courtyard and there is a granite plinth with a relief phallus.

Returning by the same path, the visitor follows the wall of Triarius south, east of the Palaestra of the Lake, the Lake itself, and the Agora of the Italians. Along this route outside the northeastern corner of the Agora of the Italians, one encounters a small Archaic temple (**66**), with an altar to the west. The temple has been wrongly attributed to Anios, mythical King of Delos. On the eastern face of the wall of Triarius, just before the southeastern corner of the Agora of the Italians, is a temple built probably at the end of the 2nd century BC, dedicated to an unknown deity, known as the temple of Promachonas (**67**). It comprises a large trapezium-shaped courtyard with a four-column Doric peristyle temple in the western section of the

39

shrine. Deep inside the sekos survives a votive statue base made of blue marble, probably that of a female deity. In front of the temple was a large rectangular altar.

The Stadium Quarter

At the point where the path between the Wall of Triarius and the Agora of the Italians ends, the visitor with a bit of time to spare can turn east and then immediately northeast and visit the Stadium quarter (**68**).

The first building one comes across on the left, even before reaching the boundaries of the so-called Stadium quarter, is an Archaic temple, founded at the beginning of the 6th century BC. This is the Archegesion (**69**), a temple dedicated to the Archegetes Anios, the mythical settler and first King of Delos thought to have been son and priest of Apollo. He was venerated as a hero and worshiped only by the island's inhabitants. His myth also contains evidence connected to agriculture; his three daughters with the symbolic names Spermo, Oino, Elaio, received the ability to produce wheat, wine, and oil from Dionysus. The sanctuary includes a row of adjacent rooms, known from inscriptions as the 'houses of the Archegesion', which were probably used for symposiums. The central room was built in the first half of the 6th century BC and its eastern wall is a prime example of Archaic Delian wall masonry. To the west survives the Temenos of the Archegetes, whose paved square is a Hellenistic variation of the original. During the 6th and 5th centuries BC it may have been an enclosed rectangular space with stoas on all four sides and a smaller square in the centre with an altar, the 'escharon', a hearth associated with the worship of chthonic deities to whom animal sacrifices, totally burnt, were offered. Around the 1st century AD, a circular courtyard was built around the hearth to contain the large pile of ashes created by centuries of sacrificial burnings. The wonderful torso of a kouros, as well as many ceramic fragments, including inscribed vessels, which helped to identify the temenos, were found here. In the outer southeastern corner there were seven graves dating from the 7th century BC not removed during the purification of 426/5 BC because they were thought to be connected to the worship of the Archegetes, considered sacred, although in reality they bear no connection. These tombs also provided large quantities of Corinthian and Cycladic ceramics. In the area south of the temple are the remains of rooms from houses of the Hellenistic period.

West of the Archegesion is a large area that extends almost to the Palaestra of Granite enclosed by a sturdy wall. Excavations in this area have not brought any important architectural remains to light and it has thus been identified as the Hippodrome (**70**), mentioned in inscriptions. It was created probably in 426 BC for staging horse and chariot races during festivals; at other times it probably remained unused and was leased for grazing animals.

In inscribed lists from the beginning of the so-called Athenian era, several of Apollo's agricultural plots are described as gardens, amongst which was one "near the Hippodrome" and another three "near the Letoon", "near the Palaestra" and "near the Neorion" (Monument of the Bulls), i.e. to the east and northeast of the sanctuary. This part on the town's boundaries, toward the end of the period of

The ruins of the Gymnasium from the SE.

Delian independence, was characterized by the existence of an important irrigation system that must have been used to cultivate produce, which fell into two categories: gardens containing vegetables and trees that needed watering, and fields with crops that did not need watering, i.e. grains. Judging from the number of wells and cisterns scattered around the Delian countryside there must have been a large number of gardens, both sacred and private. The expanded urbanization of the second half of the 2nd century BC was the main reason for the disappearance of many gardens from the area near the town and its surrounds.

As the road continues to the east, the impressive remains of the Gymnasium (**71**) emerge on the left. Inscriptions inform us that there was a Gymnasium on Delos from the first half of the 3rd century BC, identified by many scholars as this building. The old Gymnasium, however, as previously mentioned, has been identified as the Palaestra of the Lake, while this building was constructed at the beginning of the 1st century BC next to the pre-existing Stadium. The entrance is on the south side; a propylaion leads to a square courtyard 31.75 x 31.80 m, enclosed by four peristyle stoas with thirteen Ionic columns on each side. The rooms, intended for athletics and educations, opened out from two wings of the peristyle. At the entrance was a small antechamber with a bench. The largest central hall on the north side, with a façade of Ionic columns and a bench on three sides, was the Ephebeion or Exedra used for lectures. The Apodyterion was perhaps located in the middle hall along the western side; its entrance had two columns in antis and an arched peristyle. To the right of the Exedra was the Sphairistra. The baths were in the northwest corner. At the northeastern corner of the Gymnasium, a small passage led through a door in the eastern wall to the Xystos, a long and narrow covered area, 7.20 m wide and 187.50 m long, used for athletic training, mainly for the dromos. An inscription in the lintel (presently on the ground) of a second entrance to the east of the Gymnasium's northeastern corner, which dates from 111/10 BC, mentions that the Xystos was offered by the Egyptian King Ptolemy 9th Soter. The Xystos' long wall abuts the wall of the Stadium (72), entered by two doors in the middle and to the north of this wall. The Stadium is also mentioned in inscriptions from the middle of the 3rd century BC. It is 185.58 m long and its eastern side was formed by a long retaining wall on top of which was a large exedra with eight or nine gradated seats for the judges. The gradated spectators' seats along the western wall have survived.

At a lower level to the east of the Stadium and covering almost its entire length with Mykonos as a backdrop, extends the Stadium district, which has particular characteristics not found in other residential quarters on Delos. The houses lined the main road that ran parallel to the Stadium, whose southern section was partly covered by a roof supported by granite columns. A possible theory about this type of porch proposes that it was not simply a covering but the extension of a first floor construction, also supported by columns, which protected the pedestrian from the elements. Half way along the main road was an altar with painted representations (in the Museum), most of which are of a religious nature. To the south of the quarter along the road that leads to the sea through the third door on the left, a passageway leads to a courtyard where steps descend to a round well or cistern, characteristic of Judean buildings (see below: Synagogue). Judeans lived here, as shown by a Judean offering discovered here. On the northern edge of the quarter a small chapel dedicated to Agia Kyriaki was erected in recent years, just before which a large peristyle house was brought to light by excavations. Research has shown that this building was a perfumery in use in approximately 100 BC. It had four small built-in ovens above a parapet covered by a rose-coloured waterproof plaster. Vertical to the four ovens were two marble troughs/presses used for the extraction of essential oils used in the creation of perfumes, etc. Similar marble troughs/presses have been found in other Delian houses, suggesting that perfumery flourished in the Hellenistic town; a notion supported by Pliny the Elder who refers to the production of renowned perfumes on ancient Delos.

The northern section of the Stadium quarter has not yet been excavated; the remains of a rhodopsin workshop have survived, as described below.

Continuing towards the northern edge of the island, a strip of land juts out into the sea; this area was probably not inhabited but agricultural. Just before this strip of land is a well protected cove, Gourna, the only safe anchorage when the frequent strong winds make access to the main harbour impossible. The distance between Gourna and Agios Ioannis on Mykonos is the shortest route between the two islands. Some scholars tentatively identify the few architectural remains found on the thin strip of land that juts out into sea as the ruins of a lighthouse. The existence of lighthouses on Delos is not mentioned in any inscriptions, or ancient literary sources. During Hellenistic times, however, lighthouses were often built at harbours. Therefore, it is unlikely that Delos, such a large and busy port, would not have had a lighthouse. The architectural remains that could be identified as lighthouses could be: a) on the island's eastern shore, north of Gourna, as mentioned above, b) south of the Synagogue, on the Sykia peninsula, and c) at the southernmost edge of the western shore, at the Hersonisos peninsula. There may have also been a lighthouse, as suggested by earlier researchers, at the main, sacred harbour. Delos could therefore have had four lighthouses visible from whichever direction a boat might have attempted to access the island. A fifth may have existed on southeastern Rheneia, which will be mentioned below.

To the southeast of the quarter and east of the Stadium's southern section, very near the sea, inscriptions have identified the existence of a Synagogue (**73**). It comprised two main halls and a group of rooms with a stoa along its façade. The first hall contains a throne in the middle of the western side and benches along the walls; the third room contains a peculiar well or half-covered cistern, which was probably accessed via wooden steps. There must have been a Judean community on Delos from the middle of the 2nd century BC, and the Synagogue was probably built in the 1st century BC. It functioned until at least the 2nd century AD according to the evidence revealed during its excavation. The Delian Synagogue is the oldest known example outside of Palestine.

After a ten minute walk along the coastal path to the south, the adventurous visitor will reach a small sandy beach after passing a small peninsula – Sykia, Here there are sparse remains of a possible lighthouse, as previously mentioned, and a first beach. On the southernmost edge of the second beach the visitor can see a granite basin half-buried in the earth. This was used to process rhodopsin, known as *murex trunculus,* a substance found in a type of seashell and used for the production of the colour purple. The area has not been properly excavated but test soundings, which brought to light two more similar basins on a thick layer of dried, fragmented rhodopsin and other evidence, suggest the existence of a rhodopsin workshop, which must have functioned in approximately 100 BC, near the sea here. This workshop is one of the rare examples of manufacturing facilities found in Delos. A similar workshop existed, as mentioned previously, in the north of the Stadium quarter and, more recently, another was discovered under the Koinon of the Poseidoniasts.

The removal of the shell from the bottom of the sea was done in a way similar to present day sponge fishing. We learn that these divers paid taxes and were thus included in the lists of the Hieropon. We also learn from ancient texts about their ability to reach great depths but also about the quick and steady decline of their health. Rhodopsin, which produced pigment that ranged from yellow to violet, was considered one of the most precious substances in the ancient world and a symbol of power.

By the end of the tour around the north and east of the sanctuary, the visitor has seen a significant part of Hellenistic Delos, which, along with houses, contained shops and workshops. The latter produced furniture, statuettes, vessels, perfume, jewelry, and everything else required by a sophisticated society and made from all manner of raw materials imported from all around the Hellenic Mediterranean world.

The road beyond the northern edge of the Stadium quarter leads to the cove at Gourna.

The Stoivadeion from the SE.

The area east and south of the Sanctuary

Returning to the Sanctuary of Apollo, the visitor follows a road that leads beyond the sanctuary's boundaries. With the Stoa of Antigonos on the right, one comes to a small temple dedicated to Dionysus, the Stoivadeion (**74**) (7.50 x 3.20 m). It is a rectangular exedra with a pillar supporting an over-sized phallus, symbol of Dionysus worship, at both ends. Three sides of the southern pillar have relief representations: the central scene shows a cockerel whose head and neck are elongated into a phallus, on either side are groups containing Dionysus and a Maenad, with a small Silenus on one side and a figure of Pan on the other. The building was founded probably around 300 BC by a Delian resident called Carystios, who paid for a certain theatrical performance and, wishing to honour Dionysus, protector of theatre, dedicated the decorated pillar used as the base for the oversized phallus. To the north of this pillar the exedra was supplemented with a small temple, at the northern edge of which another pillar with phallus was built in the 2nd century BC. Statues of the enthroned Dionysus between two actors in the form of Papposilenus, a follower of Dionysus, were placed in the exedra's interior. These statues (in the Museum) date from the end of the 2nd century BC.

Just before the small temple of Dionysus, a few meters further north along the road with the Palaestras, the Hippodrome, and other buildings connected to athletic activities (see above) heading northeast, archaeologists have discovered recently a particularly interesting area that provides important information about everyday life in multicultural Delos. It is a small wooden tavern (from the Latin word *taberna*) (**75**), which covers an area of 16 m². It was built at the end of the 2nd century BC and was burnt in the destruction of Delos in 69 BC. The movable finds revealed by excavations, however, suggest that, apart from the ground floor, there was also an upper floor used for the sexual gratification of clients, most of whom must have been foreigners, to judge from the 300 coins from various Mediterranean towns, i.e. Ephesus, Antioch, Italian towns, etc., found here alongside the upstairs room's tenant's cosmetics and jewelry. Inside the tavern were found 26 amphorae containing approximately 900 liters of wine, mainly from Southern Italy and Kos, as well as 140 clay cups of various types, some of which have relief decoration. When the cups were not being used they were stacked one inside the other and placed in a wooden cupboard.

Behind the small temple of Dionysus a row of shops is visible because only the façades of the houses have been excavated in this quarter, revealing only the shops at road level. Here, one comes across another distinctive architectural element: the colonnade running along the façades of the houses, also seen on other streets on Delos (see above, p. 43 with related observations on their use). To the south, the road reaches the so-called House of Kerdon (**76**), designated for the name on a grave stele found here, opposite the outer southeastern corner of the sanctuary's boundary. With two peristyle courtyards, this 2nd century BC house probably belonged to a rich merchant.

Heading further south, one reaches the most important early Christian monument on Delos, the 5th century AD Basilica of Agios Kyrikos (**77**). It was three-aisled with narthex and sanctuary, separated by slabs. Within the apse was a synthronon, of which two steps survive. A circular pulpit with sculptural decoration stood in the central aisle. Part of an inscription informing us of the name of the church's patron saint, *Ioannis, deacon, servant of the holy martyr Kyrikos*, survives on a plaque.

This basilica was one of many Christian monuments on Delos, as the island had not yet been deserted during the rise of Christianity. Thus, many ancient monuments were refashioned into churches, such as the Hypostyle Hall, which may have become a monastery. Unfortunately, during early excavations, little importance was given to non-ancient finds; thus most of the Christian architectural remains were destroyed.

The Theatre Quarter

Following the main road that leads to the harbour the visitor arrives, once again, at the Agora of the Compitaliasts's southeastern corner, from which a road leads to the lower section of the most important Delian district, the Theatre quarter (**78**), created in the 3rd century BC, but remodeled constantly. This quarter's most beautiful surviving houses date from the 2nd and the beginning of the 1st centuries BC.

Delian domestic architecture comprises the best-preserved and most instructive examples of Hellenistic architecture in the entire Hellenic world. The Delian house types, together with the movable finds that tell us so much about their

The Theatre Quarter, aerial photo from the NW (EfA / J.-Ch. Morreti).

ancient inhabitant's private lives, date from the 2nd and 1st centuries BC. The organic centre of the house was the courtyard, which usually contained a well. Around the courtyard were various rooms that did not access the road. Externally, the Delian house was completely walled with only one or two doors. The courtyard lit the rooms. This plan, of course, had many variations. The central courtyard did not have a proper peristyle except in the richest houses. The columns were mostly Doric but were mainly fluted only in their upper parts. The rooms do not always follow the same order and, in some cases, are absent on one side. Their use cannot always be correctly identified. Some large, comfortable, and richly decorated rooms were used as reception rooms, *oikoi* (men's quarters), and for symposiums. There were also lavatories among the auxiliary rooms. In many cases, the houses had independent rooms along the sides facing the road, with independent access; these were used as shops or small industrial workshops and were common along the main roads leading to the theatre and harbour.

Generally the houses were at ground floor level, but the larger ones had two stories and there are some with more floors, the most characteristic of which is the House of Hermes. The plan of the first floor followed that of the ground floor for reasons of greater stability; houses with a peristyle had a second stoa along the sides of the exterior courtyard.

Building materials vary: granite, less often limestone, and, occasionally plinths placed on a base of more durable material. The dominant material, however, was gneiss, which gives a particularly warm appearance to today's naked walls. Water

*The central road
of the Theatre Quarter
from the S.*

came from wells or cisterns usually built under the courtyard.

The walls were coated in a lime mortar, which was either coloured, or made to look like a built marble wall by combining colour and the lime mortar molding. The lower part of the wall was a base with supporting posts; above this was a surface with decorative elements (waves, meanders) or even a frieze with human and plant representations. Higher still there was sometimes an entablature with a cornice of sculpted pilasters. This type of decoration also spread to Italy where it became known as the "first Pompeian style". The floors of the courtyards and certain rooms were often decorated with mosaics, the simplest of which were geometric patterns while the more complex included still life or figural compositions (mythological scenes, etc). As mentioned above, the Theatre quarter was not built to a particular urban plan; rather, it is characterized by random construction. It "spills" down the hill, following the ground's natural contours. It has two main service roads: the theatre road running northwest to southeast, and route 5 (numbered by the first excavators) from north to south. These are the only two paved roads and are flanked mainly by shops. It is preferable for the visitor to follow first route 5, where recent excavations have brought to light particularly important finds. The southern end of this road was closed off by a wall, which, during the early Christian era, supported a hand-powered winepress. This is not a unique case of the re-use of older Hellenistic areas in more recent times, as similar early Christian remains were found at the House of Cleopatra, in the lower part of the Theatre quarter between the Agora of the Italians and the Letoon.

*Above: Wallpaintings
with representations
of human figures.*

*Below: Mosaic floor
with geometric designs.*

Going back a little and entering the area on the right heading east, the visitor reaches a 3rd century BC house that was turned into an oil-press, which functioned for approximately 50 years at the beginning of the 1st century BC. The oil produced, to judge from the two nearby *triptires* (grinders) and other utensils, appears to have been of two types: prime quality "first press" oil and secondary oil probably not intended for food but for other uses.

Returning to the beginning of road 5, which starts from the southeastern corner of the Agora of the Compitaliasts, at a right angle to the east of the quarter's main road the visitor joins the theatre road, 5.35 m wide at its start and about 1.50 m wide where its ends near the Theatre.

The Theatre quarter has opulent houses with shops on both sides of the central road that leads to the theatre; most are set back some distance from the road. On the left stands the two-storey House of Dionysus (**79**). On the right upon entering are the remains of the base of the staircase, the rest of which was wood, leading to the first floor. The famous mosaic floor representing Dionysus seated on a tiger (original in room VII in the Museum) is located in the outdoor peristyle courtyard with beautiful 5.60 m high columns. This house is also interesting because of the numerous carvings (graffiti), mainly of ships, on the walls, the corridor to the left of the second niche, and in the large room south of the peristyle. These carvings, particularly in private houses but also in the temples, such as those on the parapets of the Letoon and the Serapeion A (see below, p. 65), and the Gymnasium, were common on Delos and usually represented ships, but also occasionally birds, geometric shapes, labyrinths and even objects, real or meaningless. The common association of these carvings with sailors may not be correct.

A little further along, on the right, is a house with a peculiar interior design in one of its rooms: two beautiful columns made of blue marble at the bottom and white at the top stand in a space with three massive rectangular basins coated with plumbing mortar at its southern and western sides. The early excavators thought this must have been the house of a dyer (**80**), but it is now thought to have been a bathing establishment. This room leads to a courtyard with a large cistern, to the south of which is a room with mosaics.

On the same side of the road, a few meters further on and vertical to the main theatre road, is a narrow alleyway heading southwest to the so-called House of Cleopatra (**81**). Its main entrance was from the south with a small peristyle containing statues of Cleopatra and her husband Dioscurides, which greeted the visitor as he entered the house. The inscription on their base informs us that Cleopatra was a rich Athenian from the Demos of Myrrinous in Attica. The original statues are now in the Museum and copies replace them here.

Returning to the main road the visitor reaches the so-called House of the Trident (**82**), which owes its name to the depiction in its mosaic floor. Also of interest is the Rhodian style peristyle courtyard with two chariots, one with two lion heads and the other with two bulls, possibly connected to the symbols of the Syrian deities Atargatis and Hadad. This house, thus, may have belonged to a Syrian merchant.

Following the road once again and climbing to the south, the visitor reaches a plateau with the 3rd century BC Theatre cistern (**83**). It is an impressive 22.50 m long and 6 m wide structure built to collect water from the Theatre's orchestra area,

Above: The atrium of the House of Dionysus from the S.
Below: The House of Cleopatra from the S (EfA / J.-Ch. Morreti).

Detail of the mosaic from the House of Dionysus representing Dionysus on a Tiger.

divided into nine sections by beautifully built large arches that supported a lost roof. It was built on the same bluff as the Theatre, which dominates the entire area. The construction of the Theatre began just before the end of the 4th century BC, was completed during the third quarter of the 3rd century BC, and was abandoned in 69 BC after the destruction of Delos. The orchestra retained its original circular shape (the first Theatre was wood), while in front of it to the west stood the two-storied skene (stage), a rectangular building measuring 15.26 x 6.64 m with

Above: The courtyard of the House of the Trident.
Below: Details of the mosaic floors from the House of the Trident.

52

The cistern of the Theatre from the NE.

colonnades on all four sides. A stoa of Doric half-columns, unique in ancient theatre architecture, enclosed its back and sides. On the eastern side was the proscenion comprised of Doric half-columns whose metopes had alternating tripods and boukrania (ox-heads). Access to the proscenion's flat roof was via either three large openings in the stage's upper floor, or an exterior wooden staircase situated at its northern, narrow side. Two underground passages connected the proscenion's stoa to the orchestra so that the actors could circulate without the audience seeing them. The skene was used as a changing room, while, in the Hellenistic period, the actors performed in the orchestra and the logeion, i.e. the balcony on the skene's first floor and the proscenion's flat roof.

A large open square, where crowds would gather before performances, spread out west of the Theatre. Houses of the Theatre quarter enclosed the square to the north, while to the south there was an area of temples (**84**), in one of which, perhaps the most important, votive inscriptions dedicated to Dionysus, Hermes, and Pan, were discovered. One dates from 127/6 BC and the other from 98/7 BC. The sanctuary faced the centre of the orchestra and included a temple, a paved road, and a stoa. A 110/09 BC inscribed base, which refers to an offering to Apollo, was found in one of the other two temples. The Theatre (**85**), like the agora and temples, was a suitable place to erect honorary and even votive statues. Therefore, it is not strange that in various parts of the Theatre, but mainly in front of the proscenion's colonnade, numerous honorary statues such as the bronze portrait of the flautist Satyrus from Samos commissioned by the Demos of Delos around 200 BC, were placed. The statue has not survived, but its tall base with a wreath and

53

The Theatre from the SE.

two tripods stands in its original position. Most of these offerings were connected to performances that took place in the Theatre – whether concerts or plays – usually staged during festivals honouring various gods and rulers.

The koilon, the area where the spectators sat, was divided into two sections by a diazoma, a wide walkway between the lower section with 25 rows of seats and the upper section with 15. The Theatre could accommodate up to 6,500 spectators who entered either via the parodoi (side passages by the orchestra), entrances situated at the sides of the diazoma, or by a third entrance at the highest part of the koilon.

The Cynthus District and the Sanctuaries dedicated to Foreign Deities

Leaving the Theatre behind and to the left, the visitor next follows the path that leads to the district that extends over the northwestern slopes of Mt Cynthus. There he comes across a large building with numerous apartments and a huge cistern (**86**).

This is the largest cistern on Delos, 8.30 m deep with a 270 cubic meters capacity. The use of this building, whose magnificent marble portico survives in situ, is not known with certainty; it may have been a hostel.

Continuing eastward the path passes along the north side of the building

The House of the Masks with its peristyle courtyard from the S.

complex, which includes the second half of the 2nd century BC House of the Masks (**87**). Among the various spaces, many of which were shops, a corridor on the eastern side leads to a peristyle courtyard from where the visitor can access several rooms with mosaic floors depicting, from east to west: a) Dionysus and Centaurs, b) actors' masks, c) Silenus dancing to the tune of a flutist seated on a rock, and d) a panathenaic amphora with a bird below and rosettes on the sides with a pair of dolphins on the threshold.

Returning to the path, almost at a right angle to this building complex to the north is, even in its ruined state, one of the most majestic houses on Delos, the House of the Dolphins (**88**). The main entrance is from the south between two altars. From there a corridor with mosaic floor representing the apotropaic symbol of the Phoenician deity Tanit leads to a peristyle whose mosaic floor has a central rosette surrounded by various bands of floral patterns, one of which comprises a frieze with griffin heads and the other bears an inscription with the name of the artist: *Asklepiades Aradios made this* (Arados being a town in Phoenicia). In each of the four corners winged youths are depicted riding dolphins, each holding the symbol of a god: a kerykeion (Hermes), a thyrsos (Dionysus), a trident (Poseidon) and perhaps – the image is damaged – a club (Hercules). These are probably rider-acrobats equivalent to those who, in Rome (desultores), rode on two horses at the same time and jumped from one to the other in competitions. It seems, therefore, that the subject of this representation, which is unique and difficult to interpret, is a

Above: Masks from the mosaic floor of the House of the Masks.

Below: Detail of the mosaic floor from the same house representing Silenus dancing to the music of a flutist sitting on a rock.

Above: The mosaic of Dionysus from the House of the Masks (EfA / Ph. Collet).

Below: Detail of mosaic floor representing Dionysus on a large feline.

divine contest, which Dionysus won, as the dolphin carrying the rider with the thyrsos holds a wreath in its mouth. Based on this interpretation scholars believe that this strange representation was designed to glorify Dionysus, something evident in other Delian mosaics. This mosaic is noteworthy for another reason: it is one of only five or six signed ancient Greek mosaics from the period between the 4th and the 1st centuries BC.

The path ends to the east on a higher plateau, at the southern end of which is the start of a stepped route that takes the visitor to the summit of Mt. Cynthus. At the start of the steps on the right are the remains of the temple of Agathe Tyche (**89**), which was later dedicated to the worship of Arsinoe Philadelphus, sister-wife of King Ptolemy II Philadelphus. The temple's liturgical vessels are described in detail in lists dating from the Athenian period, something that helped to show that the rare and beautiful 3rd century BC Alexandrian bronze relief that depicts Artemis assisted by two Satyrs worshipping before an altar with two lit torches found in Crete originated here. Midway along its western side the temple had a small staircase leading to a courtyard between two colonnades, while on the other side it had a small prodomos with rooms on both sides. A few meters further to the right is the impressive andron (natural rock shelter), the Temple of Hercules (**90**), considered to be the oldest site of Apollo's worship on Delos. The andron comprises a crack in the natural rock covered by a pitched roof of giant granite plaques, which, however, leave its deepest part uncovered. At the cave's entrance there was a sacrificial pit with a statue of Hercules at its centre. In front of the statue were white marble offering tables. On the north and south sides of the plateau outside the cave were two tables for ceremonial banquets. A small white marble construction at the centre of the plateau must have been an altar base. The temple was founded during the Hellenistic period, possibly during the reign of Ptolemy II in honour of Hercules, the king's mythical ancestor.

After the andron, the visitor's next stop is at the summit of Cynthus, Delos' sacred mountain where, apart from the 3rd millennium BC circular huts/dwellings that were abandoned during the 2nd millennium BC, one also comes across the temple of Zeus Cynthius and Athena Cynthia. Worship here dates from the Archaic period. The Cynthion (**91**), a complex with a four Doric column propylaion of white marble, now missing, which led to an open level space, was built during the Hellenistic period. In the northern part of this plateau the visitor can make out the ruins of two "oikoi" (houses). The easternmost was obviously dedicated to the Zeus Cynthius mentioned in inscriptions and the neighbouring one to Athena. These oikoi were Ionic two-columned temples with pilasters and, according to 3rd and 2nd century BC records, were used for ceremonial banquets and had been used as dinning rooms with twelve *anaklindra* (couches) and tables.

On the southeastern edge of the summit of Cynthus the sparse remains of a temple, though not of Greek type, can be identified thanks to a 1st century BC votive offering dedicated to Zeus Hypsistos (**92**). It was not dedicated to Greek Zeus but to the god Vaal. From this remote sanctuary it is worth exploring the other slopes of Cynthus, particularly the north – northwestern slopes, in order to appreciate Delos' multicultural diversity during the Hellenistic period. A rather rough path leads from the Cynthion's propylaion east to the temple of the gods of Askalon dedicated by

Above: The House of the Dolphins with its atrium from the SW.
Below: Detail of the mosaic floor from the House of the Dolphins.

Above: View of the area
of Cynthus from the NW.

Below: The andron,
temple of Hercules
on Cynthus.

the banker Filostratos of Askalon in Palestine to the gods of his country, in particular Astarte, the Palestinian Ourania Aphrodite, and Poseidon Askalon. The temple is an eastern type with an open courtyard to the east and a type of narrow terrace (level area) along its three other sides. From here, on the eastern slope of Cynthus, further down to the east, almost below the temple of Zeus Hypsistos, was the Temple of Artemis Locheia, patron of the family and birth. This temple is on a north-south axis and faces north with a north entrance, opposite which stood the statue of the goddess in the interior. Many reliefs connected to the theme of the family found in this temple confirmed its identification.

Returning to the temple of the gods of Askalon and heading to the northwest is a rock with a 5th century BC inscription: *Leto's boundary*. This means that it was the boundary of a piece of land belonging to someone called Leto. It has not been possible to identify this property. To the north-northwest of this rock stretch thirteen temples, all of which are outdoor and Semitic in type. Most cannot be connected to specific deities, although a few have been identified as dedicated mainly to local gods. On the other slopes of Cynthus are more smaller temples such as that of Artemis Locheia but also others dedicated to foreign deities, i.e. the temple of the gods of Askalon (**93**), Zeus Hypsistos etc.

After visiting the temples on the northwestern slope of Cynthus, the visit continues to the west along the lower level of the stepped path, a little above the houses of the Masks and of the Dolphins. This area is dominated by large temples dedicated to foreign gods introduced to Delos by the multi-ethnic populations that flooded the island in the Hellenistic period. Since the Archaic period, this area was the centre of Hera worship, in whose honour a temple was erected on a leveled plateau supported along its western side by a polygonal wall. The sanctuary had a separate courtyard and altar to the east. The Archaic Temple of Hera (**94**) was constructed in approximately 500 BC and consisted of a sekos and pronaos with two slender Doric columns in antis, which were probably plastered. A bench ran around the inner walls of the pronaos. The Archaic temple was erected on top of another older structure whose foundations were carefully preserved below the floor of the later structure's sekos. The earlier temple was a simple trapezoidal oikos on a broad base built abutting the inner (northern) wall to accommodate the cult statue and other sacred objects. The upper parts of the walls must have been made of exposed mud bricks. Externally, it may have been enclosed on all four sides by a wooden colonnade supported on cylindrical marble bases, but it is also possible that these bases supported the columns of a stoa. During its excavation at the beginning of the 20th century, the temple was found full of intact and fragmentary vessels, many of which bore votive inscriptions to Hera, which confirmed the temple's identification. These ceramic finds date mainly from the beginning of the 7th century BC and later and comprise most of the Museum's Archaic collection. There are also geometric ceramics from the end of the 8th century BC that scholars believe are connected to certain structures excavated during the 1960s within the area of the Heraion. These latter finds suggest that the Heraion could have been established from as early as the end of the Geometric period.

Below the Heraion is Sarapeion C (**95**), called so because there are two older Sarapeions, A and B, in the Inopos valley. During the growth of non-Greek religions

The Archaic temple of the Heraion and its altar from the E.

in Hellenistic Delos due to the arrival of foreign populations, Egyptian deities were the most popular. Three sanctuaries were established on Delos, in which over 200 inscriptions were found. These are important because they provide information related to Egyptian worship, not only on Delos, but throughout the Hellenistic world. These temples are named Sarapeion A, B, and C after Sarapis who was thought to be the main god worshipped in these sanctuaries, although other important deities such as Isis, Anubis, Arpocratis (the Greek version of Oros) and additional secondary deities were also worshipped here. Sarapeion C became the official temple for the worship of Egyptian deities in approximately 180 BC and continued to be used after its destruction in 69 BC until the 2nd century AD, as shown by portable finds, mainly fragments of lamps, one of which bears a relief image of Isis Pelagia, dating from this period. The temple comprises a long narrow rectangular area, with an external southern propylon. It is surrounded on all four sides by stoas, and small sphinxes alternating with built altars border the paved approach between two long parallel colonnades. This is probably the "dromos" ("approach road"), characteristic of Egyptian temples. At its southern end is a small temple identified as the Hydreion, dedicated to the water god Hydreius. It consists of a pronaos and a large well instead of a temple. To the north of the trapezoidal plateau is a paved courtyard with stoas along the south and western sides. Half way along the north side was the Temple of Sarapis with a sekos, pronaos and prostasis with four columns at its entrance. On the eastern side of the courtyard is the restored Temple of Isis, a simple Doric temple with two columns in antis, which the Athenians repaired in 135 BC, inscribing on the epistyle "the Demos of the Athenians to Isis". On the pediment is a circular sculpted bust of either a deity, or

a mortal, missing its head. The northern roof terminal consists of the bottom part of either a female figure, or Nike, running. A little later a statue of Isis, also an offering by the Athenians, was placed in the depths of the sekos; of which only fragments survive. In front of the temple was a square altar for burning incense. Next to the Temple of Isis was a smaller contemporary temple with pronaos dedicated to the Egyptian gods Anubis, Sarapis, and Isis. The northernmost temple, which extended over a large area, was dedicated to the Syrian gods Atargatis and Hadad (**96**), whose worship spread throughout the Greek world and particularly on Delos and were soon Hellenized (as Atargatis Agne Aphrodite, Zeus Hadad, etc). The date of the foundation of this temple is unknown. A dedicatory inscription dating from 128/7 BC led scholars to believe that it dated from around then, but, later, a second inscription was discovered and the date for its establishment is now thought to be approximately 150 BC. It must at first have been a private temple which was later, between 128/7 and 112/1 BC, opened for public worship and extended across the entire level area. Its older part consists of a square court with three small oikoi/temples along its southwestern side; the easternmost of these had a mosaic floor (now in the Museum) with a votive inscription to a secondary deity. The other two neighbouring temples formed the main sanctuary. The entrance was a small marble propylon in the Ionic style reached by a sloping stepped way leading from the Inopos and a large cistern below. On the right of the pronaos, at the top of the steps, an inscription on a type

The hall with benches from the oldest Sarapeion A, from the SW.

of altar made of white marble informs us that Diofantos of Alexandria presented the entrance to Atargatis and Hadad. The most recent addition in the north consisted of a long corridor with a stoa on the eastern side and a monumental propylon on the northern narrow side. Midway along the long side of the stoa is a rectangular exedra with mosaic floor. Its inscription tells us that it was Midas' exedra built by a certain Formion oriented with the auditorium of a small theatre exactly opposite. This theatre is architecturally unique as it does not have a stage. It was used exclusively for religious ceremonies, which the audience could watch seated on the twelve steps of the auditorium, which was supported on Π-shaped arches. The remainder comprised various rooms used for ceremonial banquets and other related rituals.

Along the southern edge of the long stoa the sloping road led down to the edge of a ravine, at the bottom of which flowed the Inopos river heading north. Here the road turned almost at a right angle and headed north following the course of the Inopos and passed a row of shops on the east. The Inopos, believed to spring from the Nile in antiquity, was considered Delos' sacred river. In reality it is a large torrent with an inconsistent flow and often runs dry. It springs from the southern foothills of Mount Cynthus, crosses its western side, continues to the north following the natural contours and initially reached the flat area near the old harbour, which later became the Agora of the Compitaliasts. Currently, however, the Inopos runs between two hills along a widening ravine in the area of the sanctuaries of the foreign deities down at the level of Sarapeion A and forms a natural pool of water. At the end of the 4th century BC, a large 40 m long and 8-10 m wide cistern (**97**) was built here, with 22 marble steps along its northern side. Next to the Inopos were also the other two Sarapeia. Sarapeion B (**98**) is located slightly higher and reached via a small staircase northeast of the Inopos cistern. A small complex consisting of a courtyard with stoa along the eastern side and a built cistern-crypt stands between the third and fourth shop from the northern end of the row. In the centre is a large hall with altars decorated with horns, three remain in situ. At a higher level there is a small temple and an additional rectangular construction. Sarapeion A (**99**), the oldest of the three, was a private temple and is the second non-Greek type in sanctuary on Delos after the Synagogue (see above, p. 43), with a hall for the congregation of the faithful and the observation of foreign religious ceremonies. The sanctuary is accessible from the north from a point lower than the path by a few steps that lead to a paved courtyard. The simple oikos type rectangular temple stood at the back of the courtyard. It was built on a slightly higher level than the roof of the cistern-crypt, which was filled with piped-in water from the Inopos. As mentioned above, the Inopos was considered a sacred river that sprung from Egypt's Nile. The temple's entrance was along the southern long side, which was also the point of descent to the crypt. There are three altars and the shaft of a column used for placing offerings in the courtyard. At a level higher than this courtyard, to the east of the complex, was a large rectangular area with an entrance from the west of the staircase, which must have been initially covered, descending to the temple. It had a colonnade along its long south side, niches in the other two northern and western sides, probably for placing oil lamps. It may have been a place of worship for deities related to Sarapis. To the right, i.e. the west of the staircase, lies a large trapezoidal hall with benches along its sides. These have votive carvings, mainly inscriptions but also designs of a type of checkerboard, also found on other monuments on Delos, which were obviously carved for leisure activities. On a small column in the courtyard is a large inscription, approximately 100 lines long, which refers to the introduction of this particular religion from Egypt, probably at the beginning of the 3rd century BC and its final dominance on Delos with the establishment of the temple in approximately 220 BC.

Two houses were discovered when excavations began in the area to the northeast of the cistern. The easternmost is known as the "House of Inopos" (**100**), while the other is called the 'house with one column'. The first is an opulent house with peristyle, which appears to have been left incomplete as it only runs along two sides (north and east). It is possible that they wanted to divide it into two separate houses, as there are two entrances on the southern side facing the path. One of the two houses had an upper level with mosaic floors; the fragment with two doves drinking water from a tripod basin, now in the Museum, was found here.

Opposite the Inopos cistern on the south side of the hill stand the ruins of the Samothrakeion (**101**), i.e. the temple of the Kaberoi, the great gods of Samothrace, identified with the Dioscouroi. The temple presents several architectural peculiarities. At the westernmost higher level of the zone was a pedimental building facing east. Some scholars believe it was a temple, others say it was a hall for symposiums, the latter seems more likely. The hall is rectangular. Along the east front it has a stoa of four Doric columns and a rectangular niche in the northern

Inopos Quarter.
The House with one
column from the N.

part. It appears that the building with marble north façade and colonnade was initially, during the 4th century BC, smaller. Later, at the end of the 2nd century BC, the southern section with the granite niche was added. At a lower level stood the Temple of Hercules; a large square courtyard with stoa along its southern side. At its northern side, adjoining the stoa of the Samothrakeion, the Monument of Mithridates Eupator (**102**), King of Pontus, was erected. This consisted of a hall with two Ionic columns, which supported the statue of Mithridates. High on the walls were twelve portrait busts of his generals and allies. This monument was dedicated by the priest Helianax during his priesthood in 102/1 BC. In front of these two monuments, further east, was a circular altar or grid.

On the left heading downhill, the visitor comes to the multi-storied House of Hermes (**103**) built on the northern slope of the hill opposite the Theatre. This is one of the most representative of the 2nd and 1st century BC Delian houses and has been restored to the height of the first floor. Against the slope one can make out two more storeys. It was named for the discovery of a head of Hermes from a hermaic stele, a copy of a 5th century BC Attic type stele by the famous sculptor

Reconstruction of the Samothrakeion. On the right the temple of Mithridates and its altar (F. Chapouthier, 1935).

Callimachos. A corridor on the ground floor, which accesses the auxiliary rooms (one of which was a bathroom), leads to a peristyle courtyard, onto which faced the oikos and another room used for banquets. The other floors were accessed via staircases from the courtyard and their façades were gradated. This large building is thought to have been the meeting place of a society or club.

On the right as the path descends towards the early Christian basilica one comes across the Aphrodision (**104**), a temple founded at the end of the 4th century BC by Sesilius, who was governor in 305 BC, dedicated to Aphrodite. The sanctuary's 7.04 x 4.13 m temple is marble and comprised a sekos and closed pronaos. It housed a marble statue of Aphrodite holding a wooden flask and wearing gold earrings. Right and left of the entrance were statues of the founder's father and mother as shown by inscriptions, which survive in situ. The sanctuary, apart from the altar on the temple's façade, also housed five more small buildings (oikoi).

Continuing towards the sea, the path turns to the north. There the visitor finds himself once more at the early Christian basilica; from here one can either go to the harbour, or return to the sanctuary.

The Western Shore of Delos: Dioskoureion – Asclepieion

Beyond the Agora of the Compitaliasts (see above no. **2**), along the western shore, lay the island's commercial centre with shops and warehouses for the harbour's commercial traffic. In front of these buildings was the quay with vertical

The House of Hermes from the N.

stones, to which boats were made fast; parts of both survive to this day. The central road of the harbour quarter leads south to the Fournoi bay, a natural harbour suitable for mooring boats.

Halfway along the road lies the Dioskoureion, the sanctuary of Kastor and Polydeukes. The worship of the Dioskouroi, the protectors of sailors, at this location is attested from the beginning of the 6th century BC. The temple was repaired and new buildings were added at the beginning of the 3rd century BC; it was abandoned in 166 BC. Sometime during the 1st century BC worship was resumed until the temple's final abandonment. In its most recent form, the temple was surrounded by a square enclosure with two entrances in the western and eastern sides. On the north side are the slight remains of the Archaic temple, which had a large rectangular altar at its eastern side. A large temple was built in the western part of the sanctuary during the Hellenistic period. It was one-roomed with an entrance from the south and a new altar. In the temple's interior, in front of the western wall, stands the base of the cult statue. Despite the fact that the identification of this temple as the Dioskoureion has not been greatly disputed, the

*Above: The House of Hermes
from the SE.*

*Below: The atrium
of the House of Hermes
(J. Delorme – Y. Fomin, 1952).*

69

old theory that this building was a Thesmophoreion based on excavated evidence has not been discarded.

A short distance away along the coast road heading south there are the excavated remains of a house or shop with three rooms. Beyond this, high up in the fields to the east, approximately 400-500 m from the shore, are the imposing ruins of a large house called the House at Fournoi. Access to this building is gained through the fields without a proper path. It is a 65 m long and at least 35 m wide building built on three levels following the hill's natural slope. The lower level consists of a row of shops. Along the southern side of the façade the main entrance leads to a peristyle courtyard with columns along three sides. Beneath this stoa four altars, two cisterns, and a basin were discovered. Many washrooms - some very large - rooms with mosaic floors, cisterns, and an arched nymphaion were found in this area. Several reliefs with unusual subjects were also unearthed. These include a bust of Helios, a Hermaphroditus, Apollo in the form of the cult statue of Delos, and four phallic symbols with huge zoomorphic phalluses on two of them. Based on these finds it has been suggested hypothetically that the House at Fournoi may have been the headquarters of a religious society.

Returning to the shore and following the coast road the visitor reaches the Fournoi bay where the Asclepieion stands on a wide headland that juts out into sea. Beginning at the southern end of the peninsula one makes out the remains of two peristyles, the second of which must have been used as an *enkoimitireion* – an area used for hypnotherapy, characteristic of all Asclepieia. Immediately to the north are the Propylaea (the marble podium survives), an Oikos, possibly the estiatorion (dinning room) mentioned in inscriptions, and the temple with four Doric columns in antis to the east; between the columns is a triglyph. The worship of Asclepius on Delos dates from before the 4th century BC, but construction of the temple must have begun at the end of the 4th century BC.

Apart from the Asclepeion, two other small temples were built here. One is situated almost opposite the Asclepieion to the southeast on a small outcrop of land at the bay's inlet. It has been identified hypothetically as the Leukothion mentioned in inscriptions, a temple dedicated to the sea deity Leukothea. The second small temple, accessed by a staircase and dedicated to an unknown deity, is situated further to the southeast on a low rocky slope beyond a sandy beach.

The area east of Fournoi and southeastern and southern Delos in general had, as mentioned above (see p. 41), farmhouses with arable fields and grazing pastures with many water cisterns; one to the northwest of Cynthus held almost 2000 cubic meters. Higher up, east of Fournoi, excavations recently brought to light a farmhouse that extended over an area of approximately 300 m². It was built in the 5th century BC and continued in use until the 1st century BC. In its initial form it was similar to the Classical houses in Olynthus in Chalkidiki and in Ionian Priene in Asia Minor. Later, in the Hellenistic period, there were architectural changes such as a stoa converted to a cooking area with an oven for baking bread, a stove, and areas for other uses, e.g. grinding wheat with a hand-mill, which also happened in other Delian houses. This house was surrounded by arable land, stables for animals, enclosures for sheep and goats, probably used for food by its owners, as this was most likely a private farm.

The Aphrodision from the S.

General view of the Fournoi bay with the Asclepieion, from Cynthus.

71

RHENEIA

After the Athenians decreed that the inhabitants of Delos were not allowed to be born and die on their island, with the reasoning that Apollo was adverse to any form of contamination on his sacred island, their only solution was to use the neighbouring island of Rheneia as a cemetery. Rheneia is west of Delos and is much larger, almost double in size. Here, directly opposite the sanctuary and town, on the western shore of the southern part of Rheneia, from the Glaropounta peninsula in the north to the Kato Generale bay in the south, an area approximately 1 km x 300 m away from the shore, was used as a cemetery by the Delians from the end of the 5th century BC (the Catharsis took place in 426/5 BC) onwards. Here, at a location now occupied by the chapel of Agia Kyriaki, is the site where a large pit was dug for the interment of all the dead and their accompanying funerary gifts when the graves were removed from Delos during the Catharsis (see above p. 7). This Catharsis Pit, which was enclosed by a rectangular perimeter wall and comprised an area of approximately 500 m², brought to light a plethora of ceramic finds from various workshops active during the first half of the 1st millennium BC (10th/9th century BC - 426/5 BC) when excavated by Greek archaeologists at the end of the 19th century. Older finds came mainly from the Aegean area, slightly later ones from Corinth, while those dating from the end of the 6th to the 5th century came from Attica. All these important finds are housed in the Mykonos Museum, one of the oldest archaeological museums in Greece. Also exhibited there are the numerous marble steles and other objects found in the necropolis on Rheneia. On Rheneia, however, remain numerous large monuments – marble sarcophagi and altars – with relief representations of bulls' heads and flowered branches bearing fruit, works dating from the 2nd and 1st centuries BC. During that time other funerary complexes of various types were also built; e.g. an underground grave measuring 11 x 10.50 x 2.50 m, which had niches on two successive levels, 14 simple ones on the eastern side and 16 double ones on the western along a lengthy corridor running from north to south. Gneiss plaques covered the entire grave. Funerary enclosures were built further south on level areas of land on the Pano Generale bay, but only two have been excavated. One, measuring 14.40 x 12.40 m, includes buildings around a courtyard with a pit (ditch bordered by plaques) in the centre for burning offerings to the dead. On the western side is an Ionic temple-like building with pedimental roof. Along the other two sides are two Doric stoas. Under the temple is a rectangular grave dug into the rock and two more on either side. Within the enclosure were statues, and the monumental entrance to the courtyard bore the name of its owner, Athinais of Tyros, who came from an important Delian family and became an Athenian citizen at the end of the 2nd century BC. Another courtyard, measuring 12.80 x 8.80 m, with reliefs and statues of other members of the family opened out to the west.

To the north of this enclosure extended a second structure equivalent architecturally to the first in its concept: along the north and eastern sides are eleven graves and along the western side six small underground graves cut into the bedrock.

Rheneia: Above: Mosaic floor decorated with four swimming dolphins, from the cistern in the temple of Hercules.

Below: The Temple of Hercules from the E.

73

The architectural remains of a monument, conventionally known as the "Heroon", with a Doric entablature stands on a high base at the northern edge of the cemetery on the Glaropounta peninsula.

Rheneia was not, however, Delos's necropolis. It was an independent town that often came into conflict with its neighbour and it appears that, despite periods of subordination, it continued to enjoy its independence until quite late; the term Rheneian, denoting someone's origin, continued to be mentioned in Delian inscriptions after 167 BC.

The inhabited area was on the western side of the northern part of the island and remains of settlements together with dispersed ceramic finds point to a relatively early occupation during the Archaic and Classical periods, 6th – 5th centuries BC. At Agia Triada in a protected cove on the western side of the island are the remains of a small 2nd /1st century BC temple devoted to Hercules. There was a deep well on the northern side of an elongated area with Exedrae and the base of the statue of Hercules (now in the Mykonos Museum). On the eastern side was an arched cistern whose mosaic floor was decorated with four swimming dolphins.

Despite the existence of an independent town, most of the Rheneian countryside, particularly its southern part, was occupied by farmhouses, larger and more important than their equivalents on Delos. These farmhouses, already by the end of the 6th century BC, belonged to Apollo and ten of them are mentioned in the Delian Priest's lists. They were leased for ten years and produced mainly barley for the Delian market, but also had fruit-trees and vines.

There must have also been a lighthouse at Rheneia's southeastern tip.

THE DELOS MUSEUM

When the first excavations on Delos brought to light large sculptures that could not be housed on the island, the Greek Archaeological Service was forced to send the most important of these to the National Archaeological Museum in Athens. The rest were stored in Mykonos. It was decided to establish a Museum on Delos at the expense of the Greek Archaeological Society in 1904. The single-roomed building, however, soon proved too

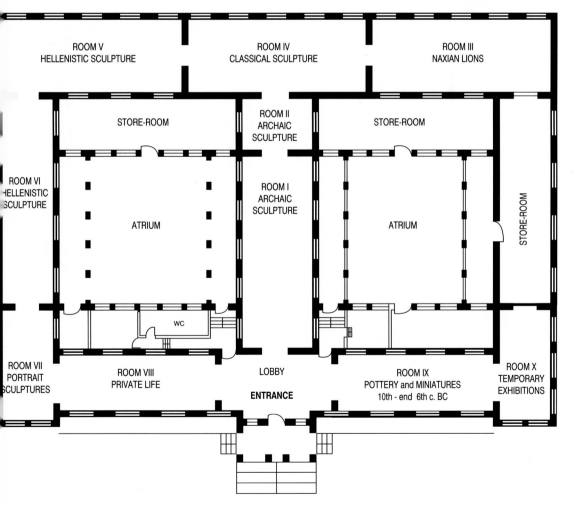

Plan of the Delos Museum.

small to house the new finds, mainly sculptures, which excavations continued to bring to light. Several extensions were added to the initial space until the early 1960s when Nikos Zapheiropoulos, the newly appointed Curator of Cycladic Archaeology, after studying the museum's exhibits, designed the necessary spaces, almost doubling the exhibition and storage areas while keeping the initial core, which was reminiscent of ancient Delian atrium houses. Dionysios Triantafyllidis, the architect of the Archaeological Service, executed the project. The museum in its present form was completed in the mid-1970s. The conservation and arrangement of the exhibits begun in 1960 continued incessantly until the beginning of the 1990s. A final modification was made in 2000 when the Naxian lions were moved from the archaeological site to room III, previously used as a sculpture storeroom.

The Delos Museum in its present form consists of ten rooms. It is unique for its series of Cycladic works of Archaic and Hellenistic sculpture, but also houses important examples of Hellenistic painting and mosaics, which bear witness, alongside numerous other everyday objects, to Delos's radiance and its importance as a large Mediterranean commercial centre. In the entrance on the right, opposite the shop, a model of the archaeological site of Delos helps the visitor to understand it. Opposite and to the right of the entrance to room I, is a copy of the wonderful sculpture of Diadoumenos by Polycleitus; the original is in the National Archaeological Museum in Athens. To the left of the entrance to room I, are altar **Δ.617** and beautiful Archaic capital **A.8175**. The first two rooms (I-II) house Archaic sculptures from Naxos and Paros. Archaic sculpture continues in the next room with the Naxian lions and in part of room IV, which, however, houses mainly 5th century BC works. The next two rooms, V and VI, contain works of Hellenistic sculpture (3rd-1st century BC). Room VII houses an important series of portrait busts. Room VIII includes mosaics, wall paintings, furniture, marble and terracotta statuettes and vessels from private houses. Room IX, to the right of the entrance, displays the evolution of pottery from the Geometric period (10th century BC) until approximately the end of the 6th century BC. Various types of mainly decorative objects from houses, everyday pottery, grave steles, finds from Rheneia, and a few votive works such as the statuette of Heracles **A.7706** from the Asclepieion are exhibited in room X.

Marble statue of Diadoumenos. 1st century BC (National Archaeological Museum).

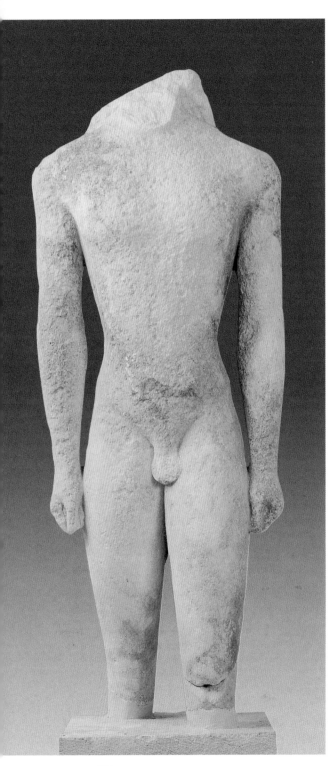

Room I: Archaic sculpture (2nd half 7th-6th c. BC)

Room I houses archaic sculpture. Characteristic are:

1) The base of Euthycartides **A.728**. A triangular base, upon which stood a kouros, contemporary with the colossus of the Naxians. The triangular base has a ram's head on the front and gorgons on the two secondary sides. It is inscribed: *Εὐθυκαρτίδης μ' ἀνέθηκεν ὁ Νάξιος ποιήσας.* Significantly, it states the sculptor's name Euthycartides. Ht. 0.68 m, dimensions 1.05 x 0.80 m. Possibly connected to torso **A.4052** of a kouros, situated opposite on the right. Arm fragment **A.4094** comes from another colossal work.

2) On the right are torso and kouros fragments **A.333**, **A.4085**, **A.4045**, and **A.334**. These are among the earliest sculptural works dating from the second half of the 7th century BC and come from Naxos.

3) The series of Naxian kouroi continues into the first half of the 6th century BC: **A.1742**, **A.4048**, **A.3997** and **A.4095** on the left.

4) The series of Parian works begins in the second quarter of the 6th century BC. Oldest is kore **A.4062**, then kouros **A.4083**, which are exhibited alongside the Naxian kouroi to the left of the entrance with head **A.4113** opposite on the left. Torso **A.4047**, also on the left next to the Sphinx, belongs to the third quarter of the 6th century BC.

5) Parian works from the last quarter of the 6th century BC are kore **A.4067**, figure in motion **A.4066**, and torso **A.4102** of a small rider.

◄ A.1742. Statue of a Kouros. Naxian work, middle of the 6th century BC.

▶ A.583. Statue of a Sphinx. Parian work, middle of the 6th century BC.

A.4069. *Statue of enthroned Hera. Parian work with Attic influences, around 500 BC.*

A.4062. *Statue of a Kore. Parian work, second quarter of the 6th century BC.*

6) Sphinx **A.583** is a Parian work of the mid-6th century BC. This type of votive offering was common in the large sanctuaries of antiquity, of which the best known is the Sphinx of the Naxians in Delphi. The offering comprised a single tall column with capital, usually in the Ionic order, upon which stood a plinth with crouching sphinx, an imaginary beast with a female head (there are rare instances with a man's head) and the body of a lion (ht. of sphinx: 1.18 m).

7) Group of statues of gods from the Dodecatheon, from the end of the 6th century BC: Athena **A.4197**, Artemis **A.4077**, Apollo Kitharodos **A.4092**, Hera and Zeus seated **A.4069** and **A.4054**. Artemis and Apollo have been removed. These are also Parian works with Attic influence from the end of the 6th century BC.

A.4067. Statue of a Kore.
Parian work, around 520 BC.

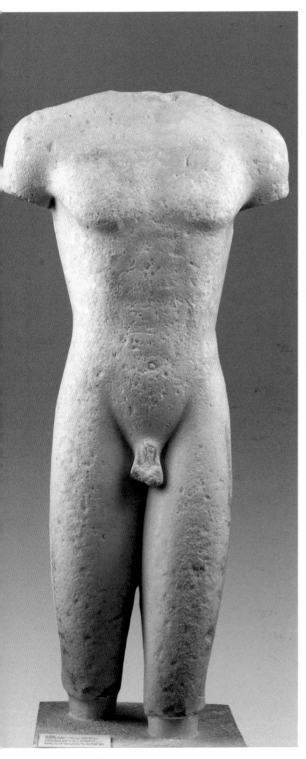

◄ A.3990. Torso of a Kouros. Parian work, third
quarter of the 6th century BC.

▲ A.4063. Parian work, last quarter of the 6th
century BC.

A.4115. Head of a Kore. Parian work, last quarter of the 6th century BC.

Room II. Archaic sculpture

The next small room also contains Parian works. Kouros **A.3990** from the Archegesion belongs to the third quarter of the 6th century BC. More recent are head **A.3841** and kores **A.4063**, **A.4064**, and **A.4068**, which belong to the last quarter of the 6th century BC, as does head **A.4115** of a kore. There are also two sphinxes' torsos **A.3842** and **A.4326**, as well as the headless statue of a Serene **A.3995**. Only small kouros **A.4339**, which is clothed, contrary to the norm, comes from Samos.

A.4064. Statue of a Kore. Parian work, around 500 BC.

Statue of a lion from the row of lions on the terrace opposite the Sacred Lake.
Naxian work, end of the 7th century BC (?).

Room III. Naxian lions

This room houses the famous Naxian lions, which date from the end of the 7th century BC (see above p. 32). They face eastward but are imprisoned here for conservation reasons, and so cut off from the Delian landscape and Apollo's direct sunlight.

Room IV: Some Archaic but mainly Classical sculpture 5th c. BC

On the right, in the southern part of the room, Archaic statues continue, while works from the 5th century BC occupy the northern section.

At the back on the right stands fully restored kouros **A.1741**, which dates from the third quarter of the 6th century BC. On the left are two statues of riders **A.4098** and **A.4099**. The upper part of torso **A.4089** of a kouros and the neck of a horse **A.4100** date from the end of the 6th century BC. On the right-hand side are a series of works in the Severe style (second quarter of the 5th century BC). Most important are head **A.4117** of a shorthaired youth, torso **A.1740** of a discus-thrower, and, opposite, the head of a horse **A.4101**. This series ends with torso **A.4296** of a kouros. Two lions, **A.4103** and **A.4104**, date from the transition between the 6th and 5th centuries BC and come from the Artemision.

In the middle of the room are works in the Severe style (second quarter of the 5th century BC). Torso **A.4277** is part of a statue of a wrestler, while torso **A.4275** of a javelin-thrower and a discus-thrower **A.4276** are more recent works with a vivid sense of movement. Lion **A.4105** comes from the Artemision, as do two others **A.4103, A.4104** (currently removed)**,** which are a little older, dating from the transition between the 6th and 5th centuries BC. The statue of Athena with a snake (Hygeia) **A.7780** stood at the Propylaea. It belongs to the Severe style, a work by Pyrros, but was probably created in 430 BC, after the statue of the goddess on the Acropolis.

The left side of the room is dominated by the acroteria, which date from approximately 420 BC, from the Temple of the Athenians. In the middle is sculptural group **A.4287** depicting Boreas abducting Oreithyia, the central acroterion of the eastern pediment. The acroterion from the western side depicts Eos grasping Cephalus **A.4282,** but is only fragmentarily preserved. The corner acroteria **A.4279** and **A.4280** depict running kores. Altar base **A.3197-A.3198** depicts Leto or Artemis, and dates from the end of the 5th century BC. The beautiful relief **A.3193** shows Artemis Lochia with a female figure and dates from the last decades of the 5th century BC. It is probably an Attic work, although the influence of Parian workshops cannot be ruled out.

A.1741. Statue of a Kouros. Parian work,
third quarter of the 6th century BC.

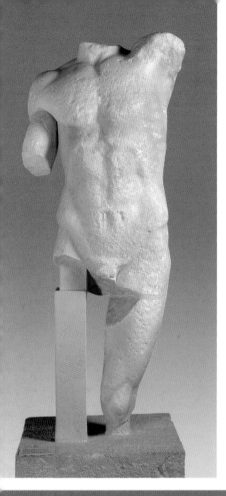

◀ A.4276. Torso of a Discus-Thrower. Work with Parian influences, second quarter of the 5th century BC.

▾ A.4098. Statue of a Rider. Parian work, second half of the 6th century BC.

▸ A.4287. Statue group depicting Boreas and Oreithyia. Acroterion from the temple of the Athenians. Last quarter of the 5th century BC.

Room V: Hellenistic sculpture

In the next room on the right are copies of works of the classical period. Hermes **A.7756** was placed at the Propylaea in 341/0 BC. It is based on the Hermes of Alcamenes, which was placed on the Athenian Acropolis shortly after the middle of the 5th century BC. More recent, from 430-20 BC, are the originals of the heads of Hermes **A.6960** and a woman **A.4200**. Head **A.4118** of Hermes is reminiscent of a work by Callimachus from the end of the 5th century BC. Next is a copy of a work by Praxiteles, statue **A.2937** of a female figure of the so-called Small Heracleiotissa type. Male torso **A.4145** also belongs to the artistic circle of Praxiteles. Also, a base inscribed *[Πραξι]τέλης ἀποίησε (Praxiteles made this)* was found on Delos. The original version of female statue **A.4289** also dates from approximately 300 BC.

On the opposite side on the left is a series of works characteristic of Hellenistic sculpture after the middle of the 2nd century BC. Archaistic relief **A.9** depicts Hermes leading Athena, Apollo and Artemis. The Hermes **A.5594**, next to **A.7756**, is an example of the types predominant in the Hellenistic period. Of the five sculptures found with it, which may have come from the theatre, Apollo **A.4125** is of a type similar to the relief of Archelaos from Priene, known as the Apotheosis of Homer (2nd century BC). Leto **A.4127** copies the Kephisodotus Eirene (Peace) of the 4th century BC. The remainder represents Artemis **A.4126**, a

◄ A.4289. Statue of a Nymph. Hellenistic copy of a work from the first half of the 4th century BC.

▶ A.4126. Statue of Artemis. Hellenistic work based on a 5th century BC original.

▶ A.4135. Statue of Apollo. Second half of the 2nd century BC (?).

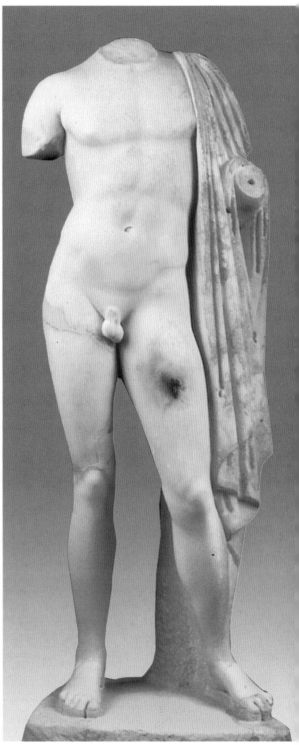

89

Muse **A.4128**, and perhaps Tyche **A.4129**. Next come statues of gods: Apollo **A.4135**, Aphrodite **A.4157**, which is a Praxitelian type, and Artemis **A.410**. Veiled head **A.4185** may also belong at to a statue of a goddess. The three statues of the Muses, Polymnia **A.351**, Terpsichore dancing **A.4131**, and Muse **A.4132** sitting on a rock are all copies of statues by Filiskos of Rhodes. Sculptural group **A.449**, which depicts Artemis with a deer and is characterized by a lively sense of movement, survives almost intact.

The second section on the right hand side is a series of works that bear the influence of Alexandrian art and its tendencies. The most important of these, statue **A.4121** of Dionysus seated on a throne and of the actors impersonating Papposilenus, **A.4122** and **A.4123**, come from the Stoivadeion. A third statue of Papposilenus depicts him holding the infant Dionysus, **A.4143** and **A.7367**. The Dionysian cycle continues with other statues, such as the Satyr with syrinx **A.4138** or wineskin **A.4139**, hermaic stele **A.4267** with head of a young Satyr, on the left near **A.9** a shepherd or Satyr with spring represented by the statuette **A.285**. Statuette **A.4158** of a child may represent Eros; statuette **A.4140** also depicts a child. The series of works under Alexandrian influence concludes with the depictions of Arpocrates, **A.4262** and **A.4260**, and ends in hermaic steles.

A Syrian influence can be observed in head **A.248** of a goddess and statue **A.4156** of a naked Nymph, which could depict Amymone from a group representing her wedding to Poseidon according to a myth from Beirut, to the left of the entrance to room VI. Hermaic stele **A.350** with the hermaphrodite figure of Priapos points to influence from Asia Minor.

A.4129. Statue of Tyche (?). End of the 2nd century BC. Liberal copy of a work from the second half of the 4th century BC.

▲ *A.4118+7815. Head of bearded Hermes. Archaistic work from the beginning of the 1st century BC, influenced by an original from the end of the 5th century BC.*

▸ *A.351. Statue of the Muse Polymnia. Hellenistic work, 2nd century BC. Based on a similar work, possibly from the 3rd century BC.*

The entire narrow wall of the room is covered with magnificent mosaic floor **B.17947** from a house of the «Nisis» of the Jewels (see above, p. 35). The central scene represents Athena and Hermes with a seated female figure between them.

91

▲ A.248. *Head from a statue of a goddess. Hellenistic work with Syrian influences.*

▸ A.449. *Statue of Artemis with a deer. Second half of the 2nd century BC.*

A.4122. Statue of an actor as
Papposilenus. Hellenistic work, second
half of the 2nd century BC.

A.350. Hermaic stele with the figure of the
hermaphrodite Priapos. End of the 2nd – beginning
of the 1st century BC.

94

B.17947. Mosaic floor from the «Nisis» of the Jewels, with details of the masks from the frame.
End of the 2nd – beginning of the 1st century BC.

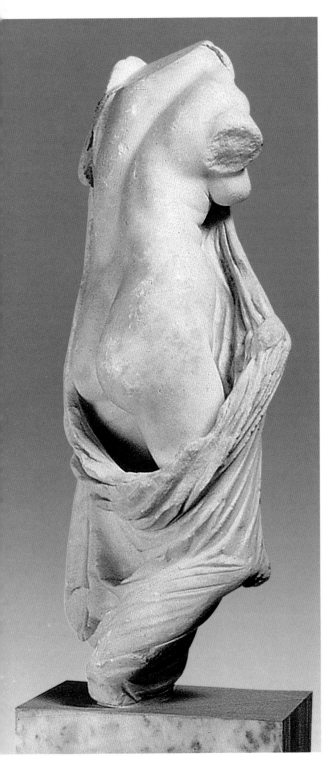

Room VI: Hellenistic sculpture

With few exceptions, this room contains mainly large statues. 4th century BC Hermes **A.7759** on the right comes from the Prytaneion. All the other statues date from the Hellenistic period apart from two Roman examples. Along the right hand long wall of the room is unfinished head **A.4023** of Asclepius. The next head along, **A.4180**, may come from a statue of Sarapis, although it has also been suggested that it depicts a Hellenistic ruler. Female torso **A.4171** adheres to the 4th century BC style and adjacent head **A.7493** may join it. Statue **A.1992** depicts Apollo. Many of the next works are portraits of historical figures or relate to historical events. Colossal head **A.4184**, according to some scholars, depicts Alexander; others suggest Demetrius Poliorcetes. Its date also varies from the beginning of the 3rd century BC to later in the Hellenistic period. Round base **A.7762**, with relief representations of Macedonian weapons (greaves, helmets and swords), is related to the art of Pergamum. Head **A.4195** of a Gaul and statue **A.4124** of Apollo standing on Galatian shields refer to the struggle of the Pergamum kings against the Gauls during the 3rd century BC; the statue of the god is the Lycian Apollo type. Small statuette **A.4133** represents Apollo Kitharodos (kithara-player) seated on a throne. It could be a marble version of the bronze statue whose inscribed base found at the Gymnasium names Manditheos and Aristeas, the master and deputy master of the Gymnasium, as its dedicators. Head **A.7403** refers to Egypt and depicts a prince of the Lagid dynasty. Other works refer to the King of

A.4156. Statue of a Nymph. Hellenistic work with Syrian influence.

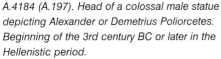

A.4184 (A.197). Head of a colossal male statue depicting Alexander or Demetrius Poliorcetes. Beginning of the 3rd century BC or later in the Hellenistic period.

A.4195. Head of a statue of a Galatian. Second half of the 2nd century BC.

Pontus Mithridates VI and his wars. Head **A.4192**, from the monument of Mithridates, comes from the offering presented by the priest Helianax in 101/0 BC and represents the general Diophantus. Statue **A.4269** may belong to the same offering; it is an idealized depiction of one of Mithridates's generals. Statue **A.4173** of a general is thought to represent Mithridates himself. Other statues of 1st century BC generals are torso **A.4242** and equestrian work **A.2229**. Head **A.4181** is thought to represent Augustus and portrait bust **A.7779** is of Marcus Aurelius.

There are also numerous statues of Delian inhabitants, which often come from private homes. This room contains portrait busts **A.4172**, **A.7754** (on the left), and figure with garment **A.4253**. The statue of Cleopatra and her husband Dioscurides, **A.7763**, **A.7997a**, and **A.7799**, stood in the peristyle courtyard of their home in the Theatre Quarter. They are the work of an Athenian sculptor and, according to the votive inscription on the base, date from 137 BC. The room is dominated by the oversized statue of Gaius Ofellius Ferus, **A.4340**, which was found at the Agora of the Italians. It is a work of Athenian sculptors Dionysus and Timarchidas in the 4th century BC Hermes style and dates from approximately 100 BC. Most exiting in this room, toward room VII on the right hand doorpost, is the wonderful bronze relief,

A.1719, which is very important because it is among very few works of this type to survive from the end of the 3rd century BC. It is placed on a large marble stele and, according to scholars, comes from the sanctuary of Agathe Tyche (see above, p. 58). A work of Alexandrian influence, it depicts Artemis in a ceremonial act holding two torches above an altar. She is assisted by two satyrs, one feeds the fire and the other carries an oinochoe and a basket of offerings. This unusual scene may be related to the worship of Artemis and Dionysus.

◄ *A.4124. Statue of Apollo trampling of Galatian shields. 2nd century BC.*

▲ *A.7763+7799+7997a. Statue of a couple, the Athenian Cleopatra and her husband Dioscurides. 138/137 BC.*

Room VII: Portrait sculptures

The next smaller room contains portrait sculptures of the inhabitants of Delos from the end of the 2nd century BC to the first decades of the 1st century BC. Statues **A.4142** and **A.4136** survive intact.

These portraits exemplify intense understanding and close portrayal of individual characteristics. Head **A.2136** of an old man stands out for its exemplary expressionism. Portrait statue **A.4136** of a mature man is characterized by the slightly melancholy face. The same expressive strength is depicted in head **A.4196** of a mature woman. Portrait busts **A.7258** and **A.7259** have been severely damaged by fire but are of interest for their intense realism. The portraits of the inhabitants of Delos also reflect their cosmopolitan nature. Heads **A.2919** and **A.4193** depict Romans, while head **A.4187** shows a Syrian. There are also examples of idealist tendencies such as head **A.4183**, which could also represent Hermes. Hermaic steles **A.6992** and **A.4259** have the same, to a lesser or greater extent, portrait quality. Inscribed marble base **A.7767** bears the front section of the left foot of an oversized bronze statue, which probably represented one of the epimeletes of Delos. According to the inscription it dates to the middle of the 2nd century BC.

◄ A.4340+6461. Statue of Gaius Ofellius Ferus. Work of an Athenian sculptor, around 100 BC.

▶ A.1719. Bronze relief set into a marble stele. Work of Alexandrian influence, dating from the end of the 3rd century BC.

In front of this exhibit is the depiction of Dionysus from the mosaic floor of the House of Dionysus from the Theatre Quarter (see above, p. 49).

This room also contains some examples of funerary steles. Funerary statues were found on Delos, where they were made, before being used on Rheneia, Delos's neighbouring necropolis. Incomplete portrait **A.4268** has a funerary character. These steles are characteristic of Hellenistic funerary steles. Stele **A.3186** with two figures stands out for its size and careful manufacture. It dates from the end of the 2nd century BC.

◀ ▲ *A.7258 and A.7259. Male portrait busts of two rich brothers, inhabitants of Delos. Intensely "realistic" features, partially destroyed by fire. 2nd century BC.*

A.4136. Portrait statue of a mature
man. Beginning of the 1st century BC.

A.4142. Portrait statue of a man wearing a himation.
Beginning of the 1st century BC.

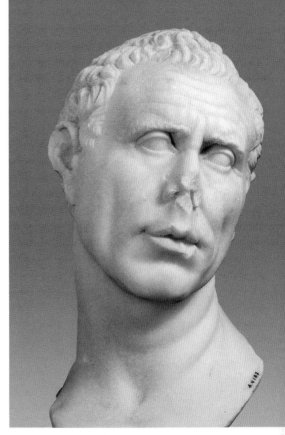

- ▲ A.4196. Portrait of an aristocratic "Roman" woman. Beginning of the 1st century BC.

- ▲ ▶ A.4187. Portrait head from a male statue with "realistic" features. Beginning of the 1st century BC.

- ▶ A.3186. Funerary stele with two figures in a "reception" setting with Alexandrian and Attic influences. End of the 2nd century BC.

A.2136. Portrait head of an elderly Roman with particularly expressive face. End of the 2nd century BC.

Room VIII: Private life

This room contains a selection of antiquities connected to the Delians' private life and the adornment of their houses.

The room's long walls display small mosaics and wall paintings (Hellenic historical wall paintings survive only on Delos). On the right is a mosaic from a house from the «Nisis» of the Jewels at Scardanas (see above, p. 35). It represents Thracian King Lycurgus, an enemy of Dionysus, hunting down the god's wet nurse, Ambrosia, who turns into a vine. Other mosaics depict flowers and birds. The panther on another belongs to a larger composition depicting Dionysus. The mosaic, which depicts three doves drinking from a tripod water basin, repeats the theme of a famous work by Sosos of Pergamum. On the surviving mosaic fragments one can discern chariot races, **B.17657**, a panther hunt, **B.17656**, and a palaestra scene, **17655**, all from the Granite Palaestra (see above, p. 38). From the Palaestra of the Lake (see above, p. 38), come the fragments of wall paintings representing chariot races with chariots driven by Nikes, **B.17650**, and a galloping horse, **B.17649**, while fragments **B.17644** and **B.17645**, which represent a chariot race between Psyche and Eros, come from the House of the Tritons. The section of a frieze, **B.17654**, which represents Ariadne asleep on Naxos where Dionysus found her after Theseus abandoned her, comes from a house in the Theatre Quarter. Repaired altar **B.17636** in front of it comes from a road in the Stadium Quarter (see above, p. 40), and was covered with paintings; it shows a young slave leading a bull to sacrifice.

There are two further important groups exhibited on the room's left hand long wall. One comes from a house opposite the House of the Hill, and once decorated its entrance. These wall paintings were positioned in up to nine successive bands. The main representations were on each of the four walls: 1) The sacrifice of a hog, and trumpeter **B.17617**. Inscription THEOGI-Piason. 2) A naked African climbing a palm tree **B.1605**. 3) A mounted hero and servant **B.17609**. 4) A naked slave setting a festive table **B.17626**. Carved inscription XOE[C]_ _ _ ΛΙΕΥΔ_ _ _. A small bird and a plant appear before the tripod table. On the wall hangs a palmette with ribbons and a mask. 5) Crowned Hercules with club and lion skin **B.17611**. Above his head is the inscription ΗΡΑΚΛΗ CΩΤΕΡ. 6) Hermes Kerdoos with sack and two wrestlers **B.17618**. 7) Hercules with club and lion-skin, two wrestlers and trumpeter **B.17613**. Inscription ΚΑΛΑΜΟΔΡΥΑ[C]. 8) Larites with rhyta and tripod table under a palmette design **B.17629**. 9) Two Larites with rhyta, which end in a goat's head **B.17630**. Kalamodryas was a famous wrestler during the time of Mithridates. Most representations are connected to the Competalia festival. The Union of the Competaliasts was formed in Delos at the end of the 2nd century BC. Hercules is also connected to the festival. The depictions of the climbing figure and wrestlers are related to various competitions held during the Competalia. The wall painting depicting a rider and wreath bearer represents the mounted hero, whose worship was introduced from Thrace, where he was regarded as the protector of the home.

The second group, **B.17646**, **B17647**, **B.17648**, decorated the walls of the House of the Comedians at Scardanas (see above, p. 36). It depicts scenes from theatrical performances, tragedies and comedies. The actors wear masks and the appropriate costumes. They represent Antigone leading blind Oedipus from Oedipus at Colonus. The other wall paintings depict scenes from new

B.17621. Mosaic emblem depicting Lycurgus and Ambrosia from the mythological cycle of Dionysus. End of the 2nd – beginning of the 1st century BC.

comedies, particularly plays by Menander, in many cases the subject is unknown. In one case, the comedy refers to a maiden's seduction and the child's adoption by its mother. Other wall paintings show a slave finding a child, a man taking it in his arms and possibly adopting it, its mother arriving and expressing surprise. Also of interest is a large piece of mortar with inscribed representations, mainly of ships, from the House of Dionysus.

The cabinets display a selection of smaller artifacts used to adorn houses, or for practical purposes. A large cabinet contains small marble statues of Apollo Kitharodos (the kithara-player), **A.2939**, and some clay statuettes. Another large cabinet displays a selection of metal objects that give an impression of everyday life. Apart from simple everyday objects, such as medical instruments, this display includes some important examples

B.17613. Wall painting from the façade of a house W. of the House of the Hill. Hercules with club and lion-skin, two wrestlers and a trumpeter. 2nd/1st century BC.

B.17626. Wall painting from the façade of a house W. of the House of the Hill. Naked slave preparing a celebratory table.2nd/1st century BC.

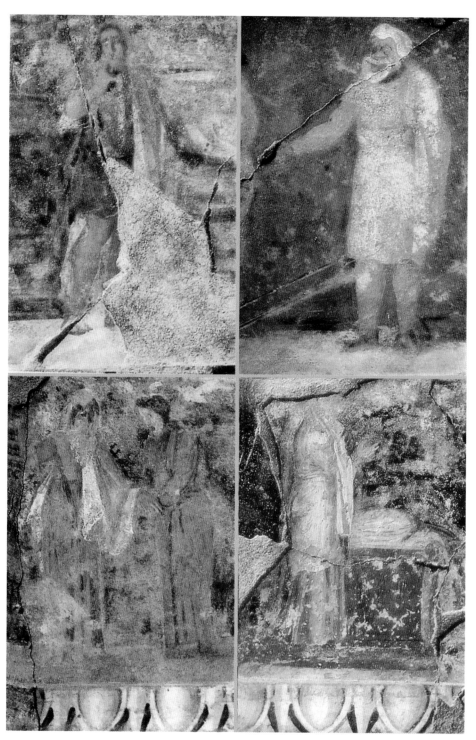

Sections of a frieze with scenes from performances of Comedy and Tragedy. 2nd/1st century BC.

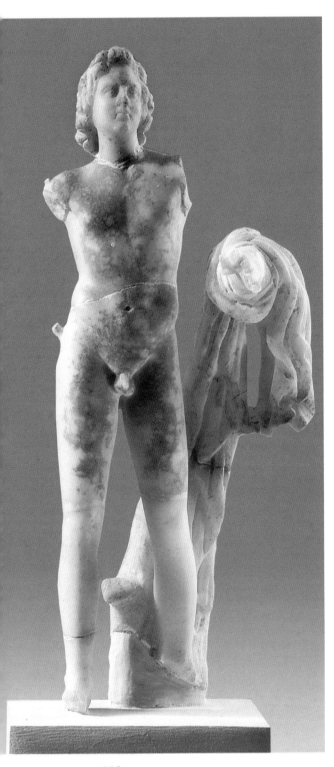

of metalwork, for example: the statuette of a Satyr, the back of a mirror with a wonderful embossed floral decoration, **B.13880**, found at the House of the Seals (see above, p. 35), the mould of a decorative plaque depicting a female figure dancing (end of the 2nd century BC) with a modern cast next to it. Also, from the «Nisis» of the Bronzes comes a mould for casting the feet of the renowned Delian *anaklindra* (couches) (see above, p. 34). A smaller display contains various types of jewelry, while another, with contemporary reconstructions of ancient tables and a *kylikeion* (cupboard for storing pots and utensils based on ancient depictions), offers the visitor a relatively complete impression of some parts of the interior of a Delian house.

There is also a display with objects connected to erotic life and its veneration. There are stone, some marble, tables of various shapes, the most important of which is a round table made of black slate with incised decoration of bands with flowers, fruit and birds. There are also portable braziers with cooking utensils and vessels, and a marble *sikoma* (a measure for liquids) decorated with relief dolphins. The exhibit ends with several sculptures that once decorated private houses: a gold-plated female figure, **A.4134**, Cybele on a throne, **A.4144**, Hercules with club, **A.721**, and Sarapis on a throne, **A.1990 + A.2003**; works from the first half of the 2nd century BC. Certain objects related to the ancient Delians' private life, such as the *rypoi* (seals) found at the House of the Seals (see above, p. 35), and the gold jewelry from the «Nisis» of the Jewels (see above, p. 35), are not included in this display.

B.2939. Statuette of Apollo Kitharodos.
The hairdo and facial expression refer to the
Alexandrian Helios type. Hellenistic period.

*B.13880. Cover (?) of a bronze
mirror with wonderful
embossed plant decoration.
Around 100 BC.*

*B.11385. Cup with relief
plated decoration.
End of the 2nd century BC.*

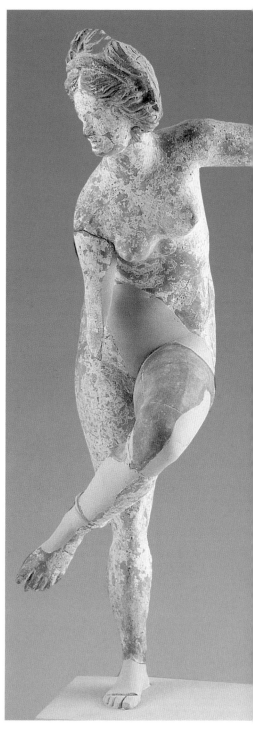

B.3466 and B.3387. Two clay statuettes of Aphrodite. End of the 2nd – beginning of the 1st century BC.

▸ B.18097. Portable brazier and cooking utensils. End of the 2nd century BC.

▾ B.7451. Marble sikoma (liquid measures) with relief dolphins. Hellenistic period.

A.4144. Marble statuette of Cybele with colourful decoration, of which only traces can be discerned. Hellenistic period.

B.10412. Gold pendant disc inlaid with haematite and blue glass. End of the 2nd – beginning of the 1st century BC. (EfA/P. Patiri).

B.10411. Gold pendant disc with relief representation of Aphrodite with Eros above her right shoulder. End of the 2nd – beginning of the 1st century BC. (EfA/P. Patiri).

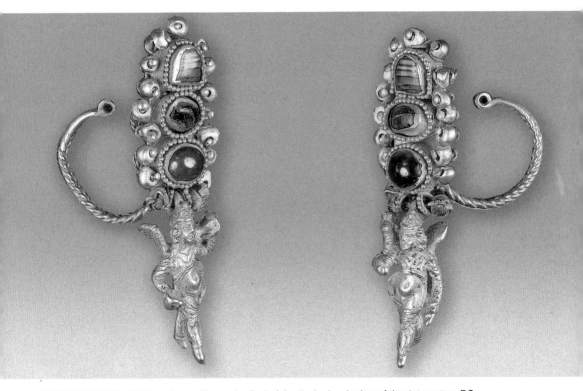

B.10342, B.10343. Gold earrings with pearls. End of the 2nd – beginning of the 1st century BC.

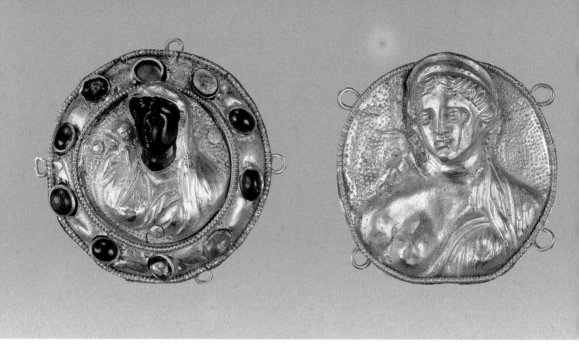

B.10331, B10332. Gold discs with relief portrait of Aphrodite with Eros on her right shoulder. End of the 2nd – beginning of the 1st century BC.

B.10409 and B.10410. Gold earrings with semi-precious stones and pendant disc with a male figure wearing eastern clothes with a guitar in his left hand. End of the 2nd – beginning of the 1st century BC. (EfA/P. Patiri).

B.10419. Gold earrings with pearls and semi-precious stones.
End of the 2nd – beginning of the 1st century BC.

Room IX: Pottery and Miniatures from the 10th to the end of the 6th century BC.

The room to the right of the Museum's entrance, houses a display of ceramic objects and other miniature finds. Three large pythoi and smaller vessels from the settlement on Cynthus date from the Early Cycladic period (3rd millennium BC). A few Mycenaean statuettes and vessels come from the sanctuary area. Of great importance are the Mycenaean finds from the depository of the Artemision. There are also a large number of small ivory tablets with relief or incised representations: **B.7069** warrior with helmet, **B.7070** the struggle between two lions and a deer, **B.7073** a griffin attacking a deer, and **B.7075** the struggle between a griffin and a deer. Also on display are gold jewelry and bronze statuette **B.7175** of a god with helmet of eastern type. It dates from the peak of the Mycenaean period (14th-13th centuries BC).

A small display cabinet contains finds from the Geometric period, shells, and bronze statuettes. Handle **B.1199** and

◄ B.7069. Ivory plaque with relief representation of a Mycenaean warrior. 14th – 13th century BC.

▼ B.7075. Plaque with carved representation of a lion devouring a griffin. Example of Creto-Mycenaean art. 14th – 13th century BC.

A.3595. Clay statuette of a winged goddess holding a dove. Second quarter of the 6th century BC.

statuette **B.541** of a horse come from a Geometric tripod. The beautiful shell **B.4260**, from the beginning of the 7th century BC, depicts Apollo Kitharodos and a Muse.

Three further displays contain Geometric period (second half of the 8th century BC) vessels. The first contains examples from Paros, the second from Naxos (amphora **B.4208** depicts two horses tied to a tripod and, below, a chorus of female figures), and the third has kylixes, which date right up to the 7th century BC, from Attica, Crete and Rhodes. The vessels from Naxos date up to the middle of the 7th century BC. From the first half of the 7th century BC are several works in the "orientalizing" style; amphora **B.4219** bears a "master of animals" around its neck and chariot below, while fragment **B.243** of a large amphora bears the representation of a lion and a hastily drawn representation of a mourner. Skyphos **B.6082**, which imitates the Early Corinthian style, bears a

representation of a hog, while *pinakion* (tablet) **B.6229** with two rampant lions replicates Rhodian vessel designs. The two center displays contain terracotta statuettes found at the Heraion; all of Ionian origin. There are statuettes of a seated or standing female figure, the large statuette of a winged deity, and others, **B.3592**. Clay statuette **B.3505** represents Zeus and Hera seated. The latter, worshipped at the Heraion, is also depicted in a series of female busts also exhibited in this room.

Three displays, two along the wall and one in the centre, contain 7th century BC vessels from Paros (formerly thought to be from Melos), Rhodes and Chios. Parian amphora **B.6872** with crowned rider, and hydria **B.6867** with a female portrait on the neck and the representation of a lion and a bull on the main body come from the Archegesion. From the Heraion come a number of Parian (formerly "from Melos") tablets and vessels (oinochoe, fruit bowls, aryballoi, and askoi) from Rhodes.

B.6194. Spherical Corinthian aryballos with a massive Gorgo running along its front side. End of the 7th century BC.

B.6002. Trefoil-spouted oinochoe from a Rhodian workshop. Second half of the 7th century BC.

Oinochoi **B.6001** and **B.6002** have depictions of goats, lions, sphinxes, and birds. Of the vessels from Chios, with their white ground, crater **B.6230** with a bull between two lions is exquisite. Unique are the coloured tablets painted after being fired. **B.6231** depicts Hercules and Deianeira with the Centaur. The Early Corinthian and Corinthian vessels in four displays come from the Heraion. These include some of the best examples of Corinthian pottery, which, together with Attic pottery, were predominant throughout the 6th century BC. Characteristic are massive alabastra **B.6191** and **B.6192** with the "master of the animals" holding two swans by the neck, and aryballos **B.6196** with a winged demon. The 6th century BC Black and Red-figure style pottery, which complete the ceramic collection, are not currently on display.

B.6191, B.6192. Above: Corinthian alabastra with "the Mistress of Animals" (winged goddess) holding two swans by their necks. End of the 7th century BC. Below: Drawn embellishment of the representation on B.6191.

Rypoi (clay sealings with seal impressions) with imprints: a) 5955. Representation of Apollo Helios based on portrait heads of Alexander, b) 6955. Standing Apollo leaning against a column and head of Athena wearing a helmet. c) Trident (?) and head of Hermes.

B. 7540. Bronze mask of the horned god Dionysus or a deified river. End of the 2nd century BC.

Room X: Temporary exhibitions

Room X, initially planned as a temporary exhibition space, houses a display with a maritime theme, a major factor in Delos' development. It includes statues of deities connected to the sea such as Poseidon **A.4120**, a copy of a work by Lysippos from the end of the 4th century BC, Aphrodite emerging from the sea **A.4150**, of the type created by Apellis in the 4th century BC, a 1st century BC relief depicting Isis Pelagia, a deity whom, during the Hellenistic period, was thought to have invented sailing by using her mantle as a sail, amphorae used primarily to transport wine to commercial ports, and funerary steles dedicated to sailors and others conclude the sea journey around Delos.

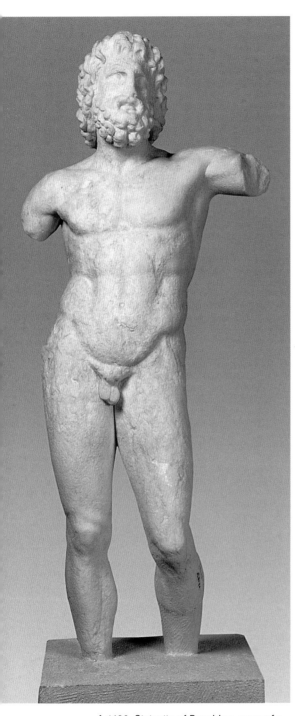

A.4120. Statuette of Poseidon, copy of a work by Lysippos of the 4th century BC. Hellenistic period.

A.7706. Statue of Hercules in the Lysippeian tradition. Early Hellenistic years.

A.4150. Statuette of Aphrodite rising from the sea, copy of a 4th century BC original by Apellis. Hellenistic period.

THE ARCHAEOLOGICAL SITE OF DELOS

1. Ancient harbour
2. Agora of the Hermaists or of the Compitaliasts
3. Sacred Way
4. Portico of Philip V
5. South Portico
6. Agora of the Delians or Square Agora
7. Propylaea
8. Oikos of the Naxians
9. Base of the Colossus of the Naxians
10. Megaron C
11. Workshops of Theandridon
12. "Porinos Naos" (Limestone Temple) of Apollo
13. Temple of the Athenians, "The Oikos of the Seven" (The temple with the seven statues)
14. Temple of Apollo (The Temple of the Delians)
15. Mycenaean settlement
16-19a. Oikoi or Treasuries
16. Treasury 5
17. Treasury 4
18. Treasury 3
19. Treasury 2
19a. Treasury 1
20. Building D
21. Prytaneion
22. Monument of the Bulls
23. Altar of Zeus Soter and Athena Soteira
24. The Sanctuary's Hellenistic perimeter wall
25. Exedrae
26. Statue of Gaius Billienus
27. Portico of Antigonos
28. Monument of the ancestors of Antigonos
29. Theke of Opis and Arge
30. Minoa Fountain
31. "Graphe" or "Oikos"
32. Portico of the Naxians
33. Bronze Palm tree
34. Oikos of the Andrians (?)
35. Hexagon Monument
36. "Sema" (Tomb) of Laodice and Hyperoche
37. "Arched building" – Keraton
38. Temple G
39. Pytheion
40. Artemision
41. Building with peristyle courtyard
42. Ecclesiasterion
43. Agora of Theophrastos
44. Hypostyle Hall
45. Dodecatheon
46. Granite monument
47. Letoon (temple of Leto)
48. Agora of the Italians
49. Terrace of the lions
50. Sacred Lake
51. Koinon of the Poseidoniasts of Beirut
52. House of the Hill
53. «Nisis» of the Bronzes
54. House of the Seals
55. House of the Sword
56. «Nisis» of the Jewels
57. «Nisis» of the House of the Comedians
58. House with Pediment
59. House of the Tritons
60. House of Diadoumenos
61. House of the Lake
62. Palaestra of the Lake
63. Palaestra of Granite
64. Wall of Triarius
65. House of Scardanas
66. Archaic temple dedicated to unknown deity
67. Sanctuary of Promachonas
68. Stadium Quarter
69. Archegesion
70. Hippodrome
71. Gymnasium
72. Stadium
73. Synagogue
74. Stoivadeion
75. Taverna
76. House of Kerdon
77. Early Christian basilica of Agios Kyrikos
78. Theatre Quarter
79. House of Dionysus
80. House of the Dyer (?)
81. House of Cleopatra and Dioscurides
82. House of the Trident
83. Cistern of the Theatre
84. Temple of the Theatre
85. Theatre
86. Cistern (Hostel?)
87. House of the Masks
88. House of the Dolphins
89. Sanctuary of Agathe Tyche
90. Temple of Hercules
91. Cynthion
92. Sanctuary of Zeus Hypsistos
93. Sanctuary of the gods of Askalon
94. Heraion
95. Sarapeion C
96. Sanctuary of Atargatis and Hadad
97. Cistern of Inopos
98. Sarapeion B
99. Sarapeion A
100. House of Inopos
101. Samothrakeion
102. Monument of Mithridates Eupator
103. House of Hermes
104. Aphrodision

- Αναπαράσταση του Ιερού, στις αρχές του 1ου αι. π.Χ.
- Reconstruction of the Sanctuary at the beginning of the 1st century BC
- Reconstitution du Sanctuaire au début du ier siècle av. J.-C.
- Rekonstruktion des Heiligtums zu Beginn des 1. Jhs. v. Chr.
- Ricostruzione del Santuario agli inizi del I sec. a.C.
- Reconstrucción del santuario a principios del s. I a.C.

    (Ph. Fraisse – M.-Ch. Hellmann – Y. Rizakis, 1966).

- Πρόπλασμα του αρχαιολογικού χώρου της Δήλου.
- Model of the archeological site of Delos.
- Maquette du site archéologique de Délos.
- Modell des Ausgrabungsgeländes auf Delos.
- Plastico del sito archeologico di Delo.
- Maqueta del sitio arqueológico de Delos.

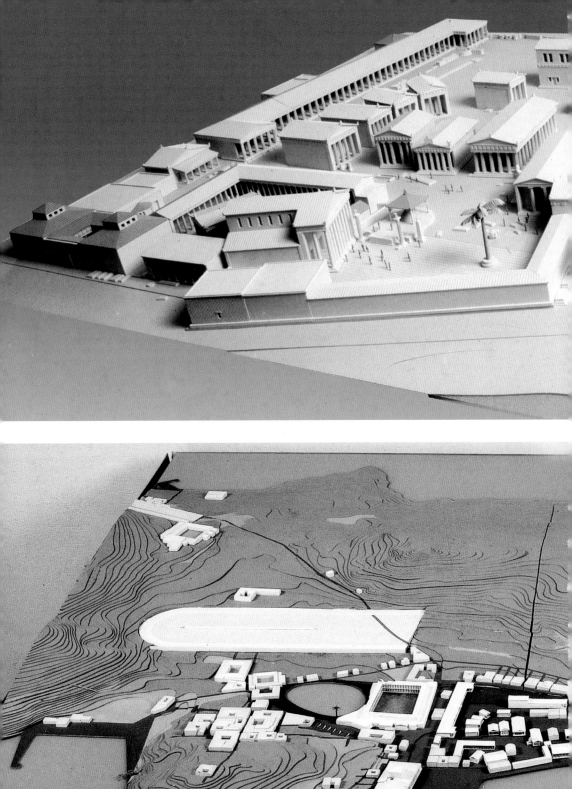

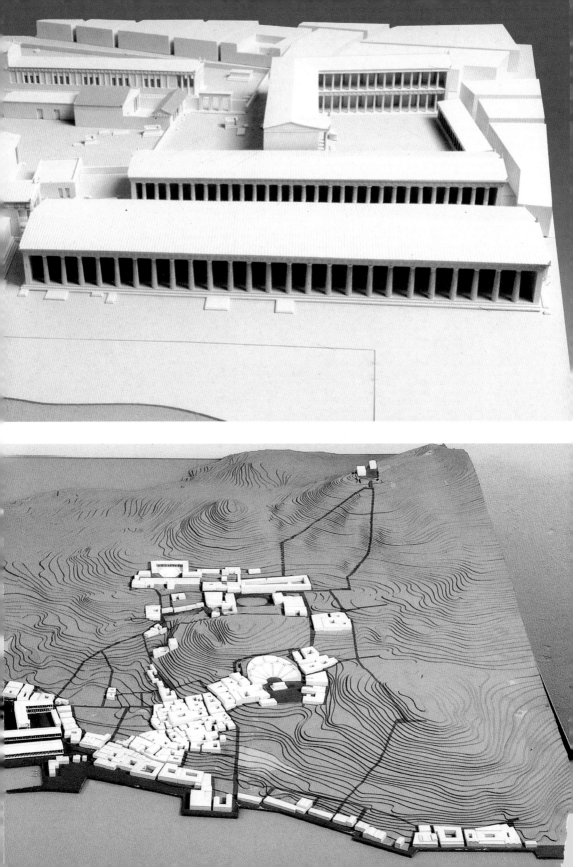

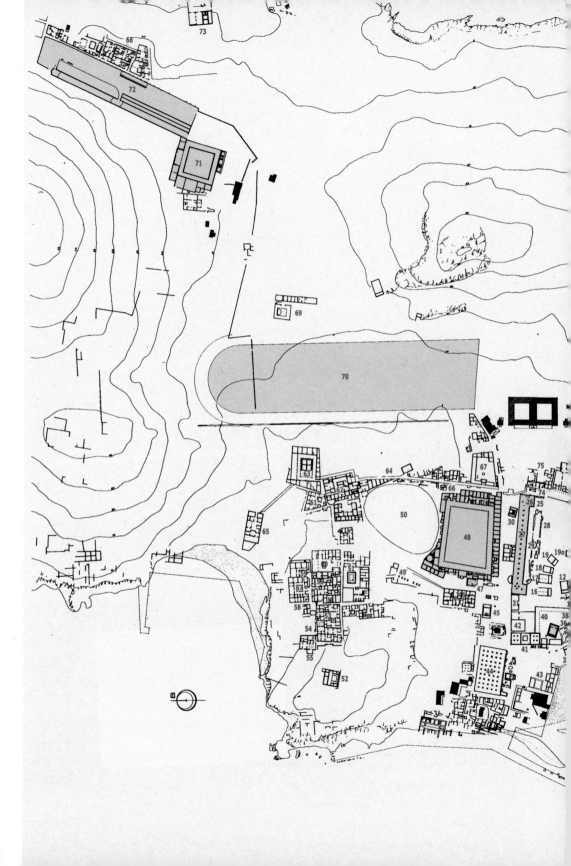

€-9
H
ΥΠΟΥΡΓΕΙΟ ΠΟΛΙΤΙΣΜΟΥ
0369357
ΤΑΜΕΙΟ ΑΡΧΑΙΟΛΟΓΙΚΩΝ ΠΟΡΩΝ
ΤΑΠ

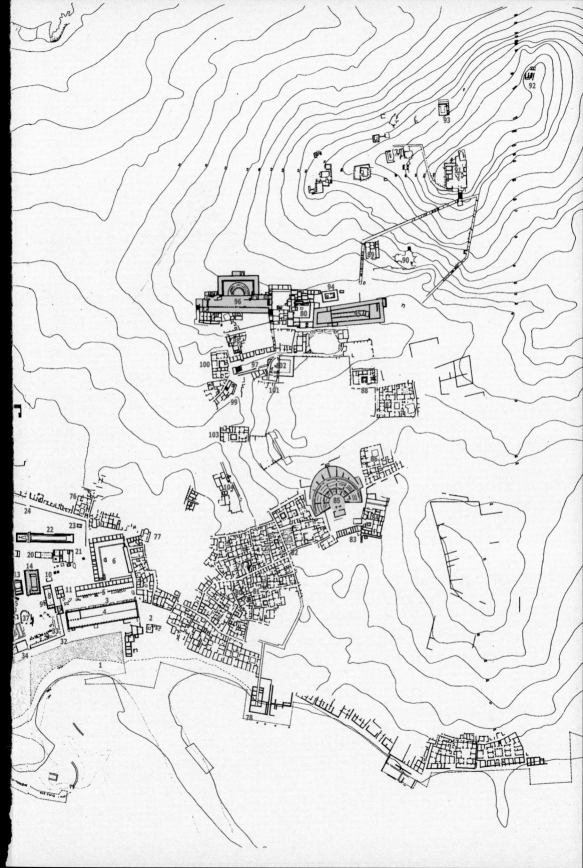